VOLUME 7 OF 20 VOLUMES
SPORTS RESOURCES COMPANY
COLUMBUS, OHIO

THE LINCOLN LIBRARY OF SPORTS CHAMPIONS

PANCHO GONZALES, EVONNE
GOOLAGONG, FRANK GOTCH,
SHANE GOULD, W. G. GRACE, OTTO
GRAHAM, RED GRANGE, ROCKY
GRAZIANO, HANK GREENBERG, JOE
GREENE, ROSEY GRIER, BOB GRIESE,
ARCHIE GRIFFIN, LEFTY GROVE, LOU
GROZA, WALTER HAGEN, GEORGE
HALAS, GLENN HALL, JACK HAM,
DOROTHY HAMILL, TOM HARMON,
FRANCO HARRIS, BILL HARTACK,
DOUG HARVEY.

FIRST EDITION, 1974.
SECOND EDITION, 1978.
COPYRIGHT © 1978 BY
SPORTS RESOURCES COMPANY,
A PARTNERSHIP COMPOSED OF
THE FRONTIER PRESS COMPANY
AND WILLIAM H. SEIBERT.
PRINTED IN U.S.A. LIBRARY OF CONGRESS
CATALOG CARD NUMBER 73-88671.
ISBN: 0-912168-01-3.

⊖Gonzales, Pancho

(Richard) GAHN-*ZAHL*-US (1928-   ), tennis player, was born in Los Angeles, California, the son of Mexican immigrants. His mother bought him his first tennis racket in 1940 for 51 cents. By the age of 14, Gonzales was competing in junior boys' tournaments. The next year he was being coached by Perry Jones, a top tennis pro in Southern California. Gonzales eventually quit school and served a brief term in the Navy. When he returned, he made his first appearance at Forest Hills in 1947. In 1948 and 1949, he won the U.S. men's singles title at Forest Hills. Gonzales was also a member of the championship Davis Cup team in 1949, and later coached U.S. Davis Cup squads. He then turned pro and went on tour with Jack Kramer. After remaining fairly inactive for several years, Gonzales became

the uncontested pro champion from 1954-1961 and the top drawing card on the tennis tour. Gonzales was known for his fiery temper and his booming serve, which was once clocked at 110 miles per hour. During the latter part of his career, he retired countless times, only to come back. In 1968, Pancho Gonzales was inducted into the International Tennis Hall of Fame.

His mother gave him a 51-cent tennis racket and his father gave him a choice. These may not seem like the beginnings for a great athletic career, but the two events soon moved a hot-tempered Mexican-American boy to the top in professional tennis.

Pancho Gonzales received the inexpensive racket as a Christmas present from his mother when he was 12 years old. A great dislike for school and a new-found love for tennis were enough to keep Pancho on the courts and out of school. Naturally, the California truant officers did not like this arrangement, and Pancho's enthusiasm for tennis brought trouble.

Practicing for hours every day, the young athlete finally dropped out of school in the tenth grade, much to the disgust of his father. Manuel Gonzales wanted the best for his seven children, and that included a good education. So, when

Pancho returned from naval service at the age of 19, Manuel Gonzales gave his son a choice.

". . . You can take your choice. One of these three things you must do: Go back to school, take a job, or get out of the house."

Since the younger Gonzales hated school and had no job skills, there was only one choice that he

Gonzales waits in anticipation of the return shot.

Gonzales, Pancho

could make. He knew more about tennis than anything else. As a boy, before he entered the Navy, Pancho had played in many amateur tournaments. Local pros realized that Gonzales should devote all his time to tennis, as he had all the natural talents needed to be a success in the game.

So the 19-year-old Navy veteran left home and began a career during which he would become one of the finest tennis players in the world.

The young athlete's determination soon became evident when Gonzales entered his first tournament after leaving home. Since Pancho had not been invited, he entered by using a friend's application. However, Gonzales fought his way to the finals, where he came face to face with Jack Kramer. He was the amateur champion of the United States and would one day have a great effect on the career of Pancho Gonzales.

The young rookie won one set from Kramer in the finals before losing. But the loss was not a real defeat because Gonzales gained instant attention in the tennis world.

So much attention was paid, in fact, that he was asked to go on tour in the East in that summer of 1947 with several other players. Gonzales did not win any important matches. But tennis fans everywhere began to follow this fiery player who was

Stroking a forehand shot, Gonzales is shown in a 1972 match. He has competed in professional tennis for more than two decades.

During match play, Pancho forehands a shot.

Not passing up an opportunity to rest, Gonzales, the grand old man of tennis, relaxes while the net is measured for his match at the 1971 U.S. Open championship at Forest Hills in New York.

Pancho (right) heads for the locker room after being defeated on the opening day of the 1972 U.S. Open championship at Forest Hills in New York.

beginning to develop a serve that would later be clocked at 110 miles per hour. He was also developing a bitterness that would follow him for his entire career.

Born to Mexican parents in Los Angeles, California, on May 9, 1928, Richard Alonzo Gonzales heard all the hateful remarks directed at people of his nationality. The nickname "Pancho" even caused hurt, as that was what all Mexicans were called. The name never brought smiles to Latin faces. The pain of prejudice developed on the tennis court as Gonzales' quick temper led him to argue continuously with his opponents, linesmen, and even the fans. During one tournament he even raced up into the stands to grab a heckler by the throat. Spectators soon learned not to "ride" Pancho too hard.

The explosive young amateur had been playing in tournaments for only two years when, at the age of 20, he won the U.S. championship. At the beginning of that tournament he had been ranked 17th, and just 10 days later he was number one. That same year, Gonzales won the U.S. Clay Court championship and the U.S. Indoor championship. He was the first player to hold all three titles at once.

However, even in victory in that first U.S. championship, Gonzales was not satisfied. Ted Schroeder, the defending champ, had not

6

Gonzales, Pancho

competed, so Gonzales felt that he had won a hollow victory.

Gonzales fumed about this for a year, but finally got the chance to prove himself in the 1949 U.S. championship. Gonzales was furious that officials had seeded Schroeder number one and him number two in the tournament. After all, Gonzales was the defending champ.

The two finally met in the final match. Schroeder was relaxed and confident. Gonzales was grim and determined. Neither player realized that they would play in one of the most exciting championships ever. A crowd of 13,000 watched as the ball slammed between the two for an hour and 13 minutes. Schroeder finally won, 18-16. Schroeder took the second set also, and suddenly Gonzales found himself down, two sets to none. However, after a year of anger, Gonzales was not about to drop things lightly. He put his powerful serve to work and won the next two sets. In the final set, Gonzales once again fell behind, but then recovered and moved to match point. Gonzales and Schroeder boomed the ball across the net with a fierceness that seemed impossible after so many strenuous games. Finally, Schroeder belted a shot toward the line. When the linesman yelled "out," Gonzales had a victory, a championship, and satisfaction. He had beaten the best.

Gonzales grips a prize racket containing 12 one-thousand-dollar bills and one 500-dollar bill, presented to him after winning the first $50,000 Howard Hughes Open at the Frontier Hotel in Las Vegas in 1969. Gonzales defeated the number-one U.S. amateur, Arthur Ashe, 6-0, 6-2, 6-4.

Now came the time for Jack Kramer's influence on the best male amateur tennis player in America. Gonzales wanted to turn pro, so he signed with Kramer to go on tour with the great tennis star. For his efforts, Gonzales would receive 30 per cent of the purse. Thus began a stormy relationship that would earn Gonzales plenty of money, but would finally move from the tennis court to the court of law.

Kramer defeated Gonzales 96 times out of the 123 matches the two played. And so Pancho received no offers to return to the tour the following year. He was told, "People pay only to see winners."

Gonzales returned to Los Angeles to sell tennis equipment and string rackets, and it was not until 1954 that he would play professionally again. By then, Kramer had retired and become the promoter of the tour. He wanted a new name who would draw the fans. He picked Gonzales, and Pancho returned to the courts.

Kramer picked the right man. For the next eight years, Gonzales pounded the ball until he reigned as the undisputed pro champion. In 1955, Gonzales made up for those losses on the first pro tour by blasting his way to the World Professional Championship. This caused Kramer to offer Gonzales a long-term contract. Almost unbeatable, the tough pro took the title again in 1956. Kramer again put Gonzales on tour in 1958, this time for two tournaments. Pancho won them both.

His game had few flaws. Serving the ball like a rocket, Gonzales roamed the court effortlessly and with catlike quickness. His racket, held firmly in his right hand, was almost an extension of his right arm. But the bitterness and temper from his youth still found their place

with Gonzales, and the star constantly pushed for more money. He sued Kramer to get his percentage of the gross raised from 20 to 25, but the courts favored Kramer.

Gonzales "retired" for the first of uncountable times. With Pancho gone, the fans stayed away, and the tour lost money. Finally, he returned to the game in 1964 and returned to winning.

After a 1969 tournament in which he defeated an up-and-coming star by the name of Arthur Ashe, Gonzales "retired" again. "This is the end," he proclaimed. "I will now retire to my tennis ranch to coach."

The former champ was a natural coach. Gonzales had coached the U.S. Davis Cup squad and was a stern teacher. W. Harcourt Woods, chariman of the Davis Cup committee, once said: "There is no better analyst in the game. Pancho can spot a player's faults quickly. But most important, our kids have tremendous respect for him."

Yet Gonzales still was more of a player than a teacher. He came out of retirement in 1970 to whip the highly favored Rod Laver in a winner-take-all $10,000 match.

In later years, men's senior tennis grew in stature, with more tournaments and more prize money. Pancho Gonzales ranked first among seniors in 1972 and 1974.

⊖ Goolagong, Evonne

(1951-   ), tennis player, was born in Griffith, New South Wales, Australia. Her family—of aboriginal ancestry—moved to nearby Barellan, where Evonne spent her early years. She began playing tennis at six. In 1961, she came to the attention of Vic Edwards, one of Australia's best-known tennis coaches. After winning the under-15 tennis championship in New South Wales in 1965, Evonne moved in permanently with the Edwards family. By the age of 16, she had won all of the Australian state and national junior titles. She began playing the European circuit as a pro in 1970. Evonne won her first major singles victory in 1971 at the Victorian Open. That year, she went on

to capture the French Open and the Wimbledon championship. At Wimbledon, she upset Billie Jean King and Margaret Court. Goolagong was named the 1971 Female Athlete of the Year by the Associated Press. In 1974 and 1976, she won the prestigious Virginia Slims championship. Evonne Goolagong captured her third straight Australian Open singles title in 1976.

Evonne Goolagong achieved international attention by defeating her idol and fellow Australian Margaret Smith Court at Wimbledon in July 1971. Court, a tennis superstar, said, "I think, at last, I have found an Australian to take my place." A reporter for *The Toronto Globe and Mail* added, "Miss Goolagong played with a maturity and self-assurance far beyond her years."

Evonne Goolagong, the first aborigine to compete in tournament tennis, got her first tennis racket at six. By the age of 16, she had taken all the Australian state junior and national junior titles without losing a set. When she won the Wimbledon crown, she was only 19 years old.

Evonne Fay Goolagong was born on July 31, 1951, in Griffith, New South Wales, Australia. Her family moved to Barellan (about 400 miles west of Sydney) when she was two. The Goolagongs were the only aborigines in the area. Evonne Goolagong's father worked as a sheepshearer. There was not

much money, so the family lived very modestly.

According to her mother, young Evonne acquired a taste for tennis early. "She never cared for dolls. All she wanted to play with was an old tennis ball. It was her constant companion."

Evonne retrieved tennis balls at the one court of the Barellan War Memorial Tennis Club to earn

Letting loose with her powerful serve, Evonne made it to the semifinals of the women's singles at the 1973 Wimbledon tournament.

Goolagong, Evonne

spending money. She also worked on her game. When she was 10, the club president, W. C. Kurtzmann, entered her in a tournament in nearby Narrandera. Since there was no youth division, she played in the women's singles—and won. The young tennis player traveled with Kurtzmann to other tournaments in New South Wales and accumulated an amazing win record.

It was not long before Vic Edwards, owner of Australia's largest tennis school, noticed the young tennis player. One of Edwards' talent scouts, Colin Swan, reported to Edwards, "She just flowed around the court. She was the kind of natural you see once in a long time. She didn't know how to make her shots, of course, but she was always there, in the right place, without even thinking about it."

The people at Barellan scraped together money for plane fare and clothes for Evonne. And at 11, she began spending her vacations with the Edwards family in Roseville, a suburb of Sydney. Vic Edwards began giving her lessons. At 13, she won the under-15 championship of New South Wales. At 14, she became Vic Edwards' legal ward and moved in permanently with his family.

The quickly improving tennis player graduated from Willoughby Girls' High School in Sydney. She studied privately and also completed a secretarial course, just in case she failed at her chosen career.

An aggressive player, Goolagong had captured all the national junior titles by the time she was 16. Patricia Edwards, Vic Edwards' daughter, was often her doubles partner in tournaments. During the years from 1968 to 1970, Evonne won 44 singles and 38 doubles championships on the Australian tennis circuit.

Entering international competition in 1970, Evonne traveled in Europe—taking the Welsh and Bavarian championships, among others. Her most notable victory that year was over U.S. player Rosemary Casals in the British Hard Court Open tournament at Bournemouth. She still needed more confidence to overcome her jitters and reduce her losses. She entered Wimbledon for the first time but lost in the second round.

The next year, the more experienced player "got it all together." She beat Betty Stove of the Netherlands (6-1, 6-4) for the New Zealand championship. Then she joined her long-time idol, Margaret Smith Court, and Lesley Hunt on a team to retain Australia's Federation Cup at the tournament held in Perth.

Goolagong first defeated Court

on February 1, 1971, in the Victorian Open women's singles at Melbourne. Tennis fans were stunned. Margaret Court reversed the scene, though, at the Australian Open championships and was expected to dominate Wimbledon.

Again defeating Court at the Tasmanian and French championships, 19-year-old Evonne was seeded third in the 1971 Wimbledon. Goolagong defeated Julie Heldman of the U.S. in the third round. Then she came up against another American, Billie Jean King. She surprised and pleased the fans by upsetting King, 6-4, 6-4, in the semifinals. Then she met Margaret Court, a three-time Wimbledon champ, in the finals.

Vic Edwards had predicted that the young athlete would capture Wimbledon in 1974. But as the 1971 Wimbledon approached, he phoned his wife from Paris on a hunch and told her to meet him in London for the competition. His premonition turned out to be well-founded. Goolagong soundly beat Court for the title, 6-4, 6-1.

Evonne Goolagong was voted the Female Athlete of the Year for 1971 by the Associated Press.

In January 1972, she won the

Displaying her championship trophy, Evonne Goolagong scored a 6-4, 6-1, upset victory over Margaret Court in the 1971 women's singles title at Wimbledon, England.

Goolagong, Evonne

Evonne returns a shot during the All-England Lawn Tennis Championships at Wimbledon.

Evonne backhands a shot during the fourth round of the 1972 women's singles championships at Wimbledon, England . . .

. . . and reads reports of her semifinal comeback victory over Chris Evert of the U.S.

South Australian championship over Olga Morozova of the Soviet Union (7-6, 6-3). She took the British Hard Court championship at Bournemouth and the Rothman's Hard Court championship in Gilford, England. In March of that year, she beat Virginia Wade, 4-6, 6-3, 6-0, in the South African Open.

Returning to Wimbledon in July 1972, Goolagong faced Chris Evert of the U.S. in a 93-minute semifinal match. Evonne won, and by the time the match was over, the crowd of 14,800 was so enchanted with the two women that they gave them a five-minute standing ovation. Then Billie Jean King defeated the young Australian in the finals, 6-3, 6-3.

In 1973, Goolagong slumped badly. Some thought a lack of concentration rather than bad technique caused her short decline.

Generally relaxed while she is playing, Goolagong even hums or sings to herself during a match. She stays near the baseline and has a very strong backhand volley. Commenting on her tremendous speed, tennis player Julie Heldman noted that Evonne covers the tennis court "faster than any woman alive."

Goolagong began 1974 by beating Chris Evert, 7-6, 4-6, 6-4, in the finals of the Australian Open. Later, she was banned from com-

Following her serve, Evonne returns a shot to Billie Jean King of the U.S. in the 1972 women's singles final at Wimbledon, England.

peting in the French and Italian Opens because of her participation in World Team Tennis (WTT) with the Pittsburgh Triangles.

Though she lost to Billie Jean King in the finals of the U.S. Open at Forest Hills, New York, Evonne ended Evert's win streak of 56 matches at the 1974 event. Then Goolagong pulled off a stunning 6-3, 6-4, triumph over Chris in the finals of the Virginia Slims championship at Los Angeles, California. She won $32,000, the richest prize in the history of women's sports until that time.

After her loss, Evert remarked, "There was nothing I could do. She just hit winner after winner. Against Evonne, good wasn't good enough. You had to hit the lines."

The decision to play WTT had served to help her game. She beat Chris Evert in four matches during 1974.

In 1975, Evonne married Roger Cawley. Practicing with her husband, she became a more consistent tennis player. She also concentrated harder and improved her forehand, long the weakest part of her game. This allowed her to move to the net, where she was most effective.

Goolagong won 89 per cent of her matches in 1976 and captured her third straight Australian Open that year. With her 6-3, 5-7, 6-3, victory over Evert in the 1976

Virginia Slims tour final, Evonne had won 20 consecutive matches.

Despite international acclaim over her tennis success, Evonne is quite modest and is almost apologetic when she beats her opponent. Kenneth Goolagong, Evonne's father, once said, "We call her 'The Champ' when she comes home, and it makes her pretty cranky." Like it or not, that may be a nickname that Evonne Goolagong will have to live with for a while.

Seemingly relaxed, Evonne displays her fluid style.

Evonne stretches for a return shot at the 1972 National Clay Court tennis tourney in Indianapolis, Indiana.

⚠ **Gotch, Frank** (1878-1917),

wrestler, was born in Humboldt, Iowa. He began to wrestle as a youth, but did not contend professionally until he was 21 and living in the Yukon in Canada. There, the legendary wrestler Farmer Burns became his manager. Gotch won the American heavyweight championship within four years. He held the title for three years, lost it in 1906, and earned the crown back in

just 16 days. Gotch defeated the great George Hackenschmidt in 1908 to claim the undisputed world's heavyweight wrestling title. Defending the title for five years, Gotch became nationally known and was invited to the White House by President Theodore Roosevelt. He was the first man selected to the Wrestling Hall of Fame.

Who is the greatest wrestler of all time? That question has been answered in many ways by many experts. More often than not, the man named is Frank Alvin Gotch. Though his career was cut short by an early death, Gotch remains one of the greatest legends in American sports history.

Frank Gotch was born in Humboldt, Iowa, in 1878. He did some wrestling while growing up on the family farm, but his start as a professional came far from home.

In 1899, the 21-year-old Gotch joined thousands of other Americans in the stampede to the Klondike—gold had been discovered in the Yukon territory. Yet Gotch was not destined to make his fortune as a miner.

He did find gold in Dawson, Yukon, but not by panning. Wrestling was the chief sporting event in the territory, and the young athlete became one of wrestling's biggest stars. His success story began after a defeat at the hands of another grappling great, Farmer Burns. After that match, Burns gave up his wrestling career to manage Gotch. Nine years later, under Burns' guidance, Frank Gotch became the first universally recognized world heavyweight champion of professional wrestling.

His first classic battle was against Tom Jenkins in 1902. Jenkins, the American heavyweight champion, defeated Gotch in their first match. But in their second meeting a year later, Jenkins went

down in defeat. The young Gotch, still in his early twenties, was then recognized as America's greatest wrestler.

In 1906, the 200-pound wrestler suffered a setback. In a match against the much smaller Fred Beall, weighing 169, Gotch ran his head into the ringpost and knocked himself out, becoming an easy pin victim for Beall. Beall's reign as American heavyweight champion lasted only 16 days. Gotch pinned him in two straight falls to win back the title.

Meanwhile, George Hackenschmidt of Russia had been de-

Frank Gotch defeated George Hackenschmidt in 1908 to become the first world heavyweight wrestling champion.

Gotch, Frank

feating all other heavyweights in matches throughout Europe. But Americans would not recognize his claim to the world's heavyweight championship unless he defeated Gotch.

The match was set. The fight for the "undisputed" world's heavyweight championship was held in Chicago, Illinois, on April 3, 1908. Gotch opened a cut over Hackenschmidt's eye in the first five minutes of the match. From that point on, Gotch was in charge, yet it took him two hours and three minutes to get the decision. The exhausted Russian, after escaping from a painful toehold, simply said to the referee, "I give up!"

Crowned the first world's heavyweight champion, Gotch reigned undefeated for five years. On a world tour, he defended his title against the best grapplers in Europe.

He even had a fling at other forms of hand-to-hand combat. President Theodore Roosevelt invited Gotch to the White House, where Japanese champions were demonstrating jujitsu. Gotch got into the exhibition, breaking all their holds and defying all their maneuvers.

One of his more noteworthy matches came just a few months after he won the world title. Dr. Roller, who two years before had gone to a draw decision against Gotch, was one of the first to challenge the new titleholder. On July 1, 1908, in Roller's home town of Seattle, Washington, Gotch won a two-out-of-three-fall match with two straight pins.

Another impressive match was against the Polish great, Stanislaus Zbyszko. Rated as the top wrestler in Europe, Zbyszko was also said to be the strongest man in the world. Gotch pinned Zbyszko in six and two-fifths seconds. Subtracting the three seconds necessary for a pin, Gotch had his opponent's shoulders down on the mat less than four seconds after the bout started.

In 1911, Frank Gotch and George Hackenschmidt had a rematch in Chicago, Illinois, drawing more than $100,000 in paid admissions. Again Gotch defeated Hackenschmidt. His winning share of the purse came to more than $21,000.

Since he drew huge crowds wherever he appeared, large purses were nothing new to the champion. He had succeeded in getting the gold he had sought 12 years before.

Retiring as an undefeated world heavyweight champion in 1913, the then-wealthy Gotch returned to his farm in Iowa.

Since the champion had retired, a tournament was held to name a new champion for 1914. Charley Cutler won the title that year. The next year the crown was taken by Joe Stecher.

In 1916, the former champion announced the end of his retirement. Joe Stecher agreed to a match sometime in 1917, and wrestling fans looked forward to the event with excitement. But the bout never took place. Gotch developed stomach trouble during the year—and neither he nor his fans realized the seriousness of his illness. On December 16, 1917, Gotch died of blood poisoning.

He has not been forgotten in the years since his death. More than five decades had passed when the Wrestling Writers Association of America established the Wrestling Hall of Fame in 1971. Frank Gotch was the first man they honored.

A member of the Wrestling Hall of Fame, Frank Gotch was the first universally recognized world champion.

≈ Gould, Shane (1956-   ),

swimmer, was born in the Fiji Islands in the Pacific. She began swimming as the result of an accident when she was only three years old. Shane spilled boiling tea on herself and the doctor prescribed swimming as part of her rehabilitation. She began competitive swimming at the age of 10. It was not until her family moved to Australia when she was 14 that she came under the fine coaching of Forbes Carlile. Early in 1972, she broke fellow Australian Dawn Fraser's world record in the 100 meters, perhaps the most glamorous event in swimming. At the Munich Olympics later that year, Shane won three gold medals, all in world-record times. She won the 200-meter freestyle in 2

minutes, 3.56 seconds (2:03.56), the 400-meter freestyle in 4:19.04, and the 200-meter individual medley in 2:23.07. She also won a silver medal in the 800-meter freestyle and a bronze in the 100-meter freestyle. At one point in 1972, she held all world freestyle records for women, a feat not accomplished since Helene Madison did it in the 1930's.

Shane Gould won one bronze, one silver, and three gold medals in the 1972 Olympic Games at Munich, West Germany. In winning the gold medals, she had set a world record in each event. In January 1973, she was named "Australian of the Year." Swimmer Shane Gould had achieved all this by the time she was 16 years old.

She took her first Olympic gold medal when she won the 200-meter individual medley in the record time of 2 minutes, 23.07 seconds (2:23.07). She won the 200-meter freestyle event in 2:03.56 and the 400-meter freestyle in 4:19.04 for her other gold medals.

In the 800-meter freestyle, Shane won the silver medal, finishing second at 8:56.39 to America's Keena Rothhammer. Shane's bronze medal came for third place in the 100-meter freestyle. Her time was 59.06 seconds.

Shane excelled in distances as well as sprints. At one time in 1972, she held the world record at every freestyle distance, the first woman to hold this distinction since Helene Madison, a United States swimmer

of the 1930's.

At the beginning of 1973, Shane Gould held the world freestyle marks for 100, 200, 400, and 1500 meters. Only the 800—the event she lost to Keena Rothhammer in the 1972 Olympics—was missing from her collection. Early in 1973, Shane became the first woman to swim 1500 meters in less than 17 minutes, setting a record time of 16:56.9. (This clock-

Shane Gould cannot relax until she hears the final results. Here, she watches the officials for the time after a close race.

Gould, Shane

At her home in Sydney, Australia, Shane displays the medals she won at the 1972 Olympics. She won three gold, one silver, and one bronze medal.

Australian Shane Gould holds up her good-luck toy kangaroo after a gold medal victory in the 200-meter butterfly at the 1972 Olympic Games in Munich, West Germany.

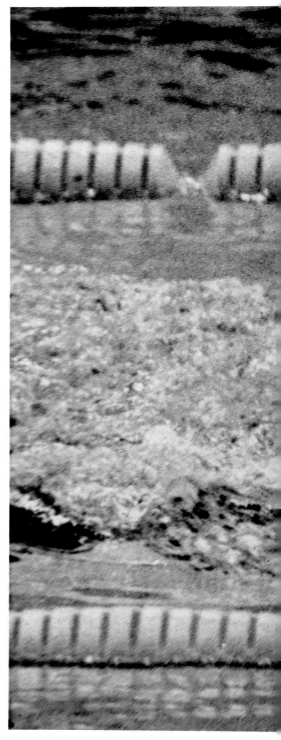

ing would have been fast enough to win the men's 1500 meters at the Olympics as recently as 1964.)

Under the coaching of Forbes Carlile, one of the top Australian swimming teachers, Shane developed a style that other swimmers quickly imitated. She used two shallow kicks for each cycle of the arms. This method had been used for years by distance swimmers, but never before by a successful sprinter. Shane swam in this fashion regardless of distance.

Shane Gould was Australia's successor to its all-time great swimmer Dawn Fraser, who won three Olympic gold medals in the 100-meter freestyle. In 1971, Shane showed she was ready to assume Dawn Fraser's championship mantle. She tied the earlier swimmer's 100-meter world record of 58.9 seconds, set in 1964. Shane lowered that mark to 58.5 on January 8, 1972.

Shane Gould was a big girl, standing 5 feet, 7½ inches, and weighing 140 pounds. She was born in the Fiji Islands on November 23, 1956, the day that the only Olympic Games ever held in Australia began in Melbourne. When she was three, Shane spilled boiling tea over herself. Doctors recommended swimming as the best way to insure complete recovery from the burns. She loved the water and was soon spending

Shane displays her expert form at the 1972 Olympics. Here, she is on her way to victory in the individual medley event.

23

Gould, Shane

Winning 10 gold medals between them at the 1972 Olympics, Shane Gould (right) and Mark Spitz discuss their success.

much of her time there.

Shane began competitive swimming at 10 when her family lived in Brisbane, Australia. Her mother assisted greatly in Shane's development as a swimmer, chauffering her to practices, school, and competitions. After Shane's triple gold-medal performance at the Munich Olympics, her mother planted three trees in the garden of the Gould home.

Shane came under the coaching of Carlile in 1970, when the Goulds moved to Sydney. On tours through Europe and the United States she received many trophies, awarded for her outstanding ability.

After the 1972 Olympics, Shane moved to Los Altos, California, to attend St. Francis High School. In the United States, she represented the Foothill Aquatic Club, coached by Nort Thorton. Forbes Carlile and his wife, Ursula, continued to coach her by mail. After swimming in a few more meets, Shane Gould retired and returned to Australia.

Shane leaves her home in Sydney, Australia, to begin three months of study at St. Francis High School in Los Altos, California, in 1973.

After the 1972 Olympics, Shane came to the United States to attend school and continue her swimming. She is shown here with friends at Foothill Junior College, in Los Altos, California.

Young swimmers get some pointers from Shane at a pool near Sydney.

Shane shows off her good-luck kangaroo after winning another gold medal at the 1972 Olympics in Munich.

⬛ Grace, W. G. (William Gilbert),

(1848-1915), cricket player, was born in the village of Downend, in Gloucestershire, England. Growing up in a family of cricket players, Grace began developing into a first-class competitor in 1865. Before long, he became one of the best and most popular players in the game. Over a period of 44 years, he scored 54,904 runs, an average of 39.52 an inning, and 126 centuries (innings of 100 or more) in top-flight competition. As a bowler, Grace took a total of 2876 wickets in his career. Grace

was captain of Gloucestershire for 29 years. During the 1871 season, Grace scored a record 2739 runs. He also scored 400 not out in one inning of a game in 1876. Grace toured the United States, Canada, and Australia during his career. By the time he retired from first-class play in 1908, he had scored over 100,000 runs in both major and minor matches.

William Gilbert Grace—known throughout the world of cricket as "W. G."—was the first great popular hero of the game.

More than 100 years have passed since the lanky, teen-age youth first burst on the scene, but he still stands as the colossus of the cricketers. His personality and his example had as much influence on the game as his skill and his performances. Grace transformed the art of batting in his lifetime. He set records that had been thought impossible. He astonished and delighted the fans at the same time. As a public figure, big and black-bearded, he was as well-known to Englishmen as was the Prime Minister.

Queen Victoria had been on the throne 11 years when William Gilbert (W. G.) Grace was born on July 18, 1848, in the small Gloucestershire village of Downend, near Bristol. His father, uncle, and four brothers were all enthusiastic cricketers. Even his mother Martha had an unusual knowledge of the game and was an important influence on her sons.

In a regulation or championship match (game), two innings are played, with all players (11) on both sides having one turn at bat in each inning. A player remains at bat until he is put out. The match can often last for several days.

When he was only 15, W. G.

achieved the first of many victories for the South Wales Cricket Club against the Gentlemen of Sussex at Brighton. The following year, 1865, he began in first-class cricket. By the time he was 18, everyone was calling him "The Champion." He showed a wonderful ability to combine defense and attack in his batsmanship, something cricket had never known before.

So expert was W. G.'s judgment of bowling, and so skilled his stroke-play, that unplayable pitches seemed not to exist for him. "He ought to have a littler bat," was the sad complaint of bowlers up and down England. Fast bowlers especially were punished by W. G. without mercy. One, James Shaw

W. G. Grace of Gloucestershire, England, is considered to be the greatest figure in cricket history. During his 44 years of play in first-class cricket, Grace scored 54,904 runs.

of Nottinghamshire, remarked, "It is a case of I puts the ball where I please, and *he* puts it where he pleases." The better the bowling he faced, the better W. G. liked it.

W. G. Grace scored 54,904 runs at an average of 39.52 in nearly 1500 innings of first-class cricket over the remarkable span of 44 seasons. He was still a fierce opponent when he left first-class cricket in 1908.

Over the same period he also took 2876 wickets with his deadly round-arm style of bowling. This record alone would have made him an outstanding player. He also had great skill as a fielder. He served as captain of Gloucestershire for 29 years. He also captained English teams in Test Matches at home and abroad. In regular matches of the Gentlemen versus the Players (the best amateurs against the best professionals), he always did well. In all matches, major and minor, he scored over 100,000 runs—a total since unapproached. Yet, with all his success, he never made an enemy. He kept to the end of his career a boyish zest for both cricket and life.

At 50, W. G. played his last Test Match for England after 21 previous appearances. Up to this time his career as a cricketer was a long, winning roll-call. Throughout the 1870's, runs flowed from his bat. A huge man, his energy seemed endless. He set a new seasonal record total with 2739 runs in 1871 at what was then a remarkable average of 78.25. He again passed 2000 runs in 1873. At the end of this season, he married.

His honeymoon trip that winter was the first of his two visits to Australia. The previous year, in 1872, he had toured Canada and the United States with an English team under R. A. FitzGerald, Secretary of the Marylebone Cricket Club. On that tour, W. G. proved himself highly popular as well as highly successful. He played at Montreal, Ottawa, Toronto (where he scored 142), London, Hamilton, New York, Philadelphia (where 21 wickets fell to him), and Boston. Altogether in the brief one-month tour, he made 567 runs, took 76 wickets, and held 22 catches. He also made after-dinner speeches that captivated his listeners on both sides of the border.

Another magic year for Grace was 1876. On July 10, he took a United South of England team of 11 to play a local 22-man team of Grimsby. The Grimsby captain complained that the side brought by W. G. was not strong enough. The complaint turned out to be a foolish one. W. G. proceeded to make the highest score of his life in any class of cricket—exactly 400 not out in 13½ hours. He did this against 22 fieldsmen, 15 of whom tried bowling against the champion without success. His actual score was 399, but the scorers added a single to celebrate the mighty innings—and also the birth, on the second day of the game, of W. G.'s second son.

Just a month later, in August 1876, W. G. scored 344, 177, and 318 not out for a total of 839 runs in three straight innings in first-class cricket. Then, as now, this was extraordinary. Thousands of batsmen go through a whole career without reaching 300. When he was nearing his 47th birthday, in 1895, W. G. became the first of very few players who have scored 1000 runs within the month of May.

When W. G. died, on October 23, 1915, England stood still for a moment in the midst of the First World War to remember and to mourn "The Great Cricketer."

⬤ **Graham, Otto** (1921-   ),

football player, was born in Waukegan, Illinois. An all-state high school basketball player, Graham had not planned to play football when he enrolled at Northwestern University. But he was talked into trying out for the team and made it. By the time he graduated, he had become an All-America tailback and one of the most famous players in Wildcat history. He also won All-America mention in basketball in college. Graham was converted to quarterback while playing for a military team—North Carolina Pre-Flight—during World War II. After the war, he played briefly with the professional Rochester Royals basketball team. Then in 1946, he joined coach Paul Brown's Cleveland Browns in the newly formed All-America Football Conference. From 1946 through 1949, Graham led the

Cleveland team to four league titles. The Browns joined the National Football League (NFL) in 1950, and Graham wasted no time leading the team to an NFL crown. To the surprise of NFL people, Graham was both an instant and perennial success. Graham later coached the Coast Guard Academy, the College All-Stars, and the Washington Redskins.

In 1964, sportswriters voted Otto Graham the best quarterback of all time. Statistically, he rates as the number-one quarterback in history. During his 10 seasons with the Cleveland Browns, Graham directed his team to 10 division titles, including four straight All-America Football Conference (AAFC) championships and three National Football League (NFL) championships in six playoffs.

Born on December 6, 1921, in Waukegan, Illinois, Otto Everett

Graham, Jr., was a young man of many talents. In high school, he starred in track, swimming, baseball, basketball, and football. He also played the piano, cornet, French horn, and violin. Planning to major in music, he accepted a basketball scholarship to Northwestern University because it was close to his home. He had no thought of a football career.

Lynn "Pappy" Waldorf, then the Northwestern coach, saw Otto playing touch football with other

students. Impressed by the way the freshman threw spiral passes, Waldorf invited him to try out for the varsity. Unfortunately, a knee injury kept Graham out of school for a year. On his return to school, he rejoined the football team and became the finest quarterback in Northwestern's history. He was not only chosen for All-America honors in football, but in basketball as well.

At the end of World War II, Paul Brown was signing players for

Graham, Otto

During a break in the action, Sonny Jurgensen (Number 9) confers with Otto Graham (right), then the Redskin head coach.

a Cleveland team to play in the newly organized All-America Football Conference. Graham was Brown's first choice. At the time, old pros thought Brown, a believer in the T formation, had made a mistake in recruiting Graham, since he had been a tailback at Northwestern.

"Ridiculous," snapped Brown in answer. "Otto is first of all a great passer. He can think, he has good vision, and is a team man. What more could you ask?"

While waiting for the new Cleveland Browns team to be ready, Graham played pro basketball with the Rochester Royals. That year the Royals won the National Basketball League (NBL) title.

By the following autumn in 1946, the Browns and the new conference were launched, and Graham donned his new uniform.

In preparation for the 1961 game with the Philadelphia Eagles, coach Graham (center) of the College All-Stars goes over strategy with two of his quarterbacks, Bill Kilmer (left) of UCLA and Tom Matte (right) of Ohio State. Both quarterbacks went on to great pro careers.

"My basketball was a great help to me," said Otto Graham. "It gave me the agility and the footwork I needed for pro football."

The mating of Graham with the coaching talent of Paul Brown produced the longest era of success in pro football history. Though different in personality, player and coach combined to make a most effective pair. Brown was a taskmaster, stern and tense. Graham was loose, cocky, happy-go-lucky. But both were totally dedicated to winning.

Brown and Graham differed on only one point. Early in his career with the Browns, the coach began calling the plays through his messenger guard system. But Graham believed that a veteran quarterback could see things a coach and his spotters could not see. Although he resented Brown's supervision, he said, "I went along with it, for Paul not only was the coach, but he also signed my paycheck."

Brown did allow Graham the option of changing the play at the line of scrimmage if he felt the original call would not work. But the coach did not like these calls because he believed the runner did not get as good blocking support.

The Cleveland Browns' offense was simple, but it was effective because its operation was precise. No defense could stop Otto Graham from moving the Browns rapidly down the field on sideline passes to Mac Speedie and Dante Lavelli. Graham also used halfback Edgar "Special Delivery" Jones for flare passes when under pressure. When the opposing defense would spread out to stop the blitz, Graham would send the great fullback Marion Motley thundering up the middle.

When the All-America Football Conference folded after the 1949 season, Baltimore, Cleveland, and San Francisco were admitted to the

National Football League. The Browns, who completely dominated the All-America, were looked on in the NFL as the champions of a "Mickey Mouse" league. They would be lucky to win a few games a year in the NFL, critics believed.

Those same critics learned how wrong they were in the Browns' first game against the Philadelphia Eagles. The Eagles had been the champions the previous two seasons. Even though everyone expected them to smear the Browns, 71,327 fans jammed Municipal Stadium. The Eagles quickly went into a 3-0 lead, and the customers settled back to enjoy the runaway.

It was a runaway—but in the other direction. The Eagles were even more helpless against Graham's passing attack than many of his old AAFC rivals had been. The Browns' great 35-10 victory firmly established them as a team to be reckoned with and Graham as one of the top quarterbacks in pro football.

Otto Graham continued to improve. Every year in the league he was chosen All-NFL. He never again had to play defense, as he had done throughout his AAFC career. This change made him play better than before.

In 1950, their first year in the NFL, Graham and the Browns won 10 games and lost 2. After defeating

Graham, Otto

the New York Giants in the playoffs for the Eastern championship, the Browns met the Los Angeles Rams for the NFL title.

Against the Giants, Graham—instead of pulling his usual trap up the middle—waited on the icy ground until the Giants' guards had committed themselves. Then he skated right past them to set up the winning field goal. The final score was 8-3.

In the 1950 championship game, the Rams seemed headed for victory. Bob Waterfield, the Rams' great quarterback, was having one of his best days. But Graham rallied his forces. Trailing, 28-27, with less than two minutes to play, the Browns started out on their 32-yard line after fielding a punt. Graham launched a series of short passes to work the ball down the field to the 11. From there, Lou Groza booted the field goal to win, 30-28.

Although NFL title games were usually low scoring, Graham tossed four touchdown passes to set a playoff record. He threw for three more in 1954, as Cleveland swamped Detroit, 56-10. In 1955, Graham scored twice and passed for two more touchdowns in the 38-14 conquest of the Rams.

At 6 feet, 1 inch, and 195 pounds, Graham had a strong arm that was extremely accurate. He had a deceptive, swift, loping stride,

After spending three seasons as coach of the Washington Redskins, Graham (right) returned to the Coast Guard Academy, where he had coached from 1959 to 1965. Here he is in 1970, being sworn in as a Coast Guard captain by John A. Volpe, Secretary of Transportation.

which served him well when he was rushed. He had a keen mind for football to go with his pride and determination. On the field, he also was a gambler who shocked the opposition—as well as coach Brown—with his daring plays when backed up to his own goal. His quickness helped him evade injuries.

Graham retired after the 1954 season, but a $25,000 offer lured him back for 1955. This was the highest salary ever paid a pro football player up to that time. His return paid off in another NFL title.

In four AAFC seasons, Otto completed 55.8 per cent of his passes. In six years in the NFL, his

percentage was 55.7.

Graham led the NFL in passing in 1953. He completed 64.7 per cent of his tosses for 2722 yards that year. In 1955, his last season, he again led the league in passing.

Again Otto Graham retired, and this time his retirement was for good. He said it was not the physical pressure that retired him—it was the mental pressure. With Graham gone, the Browns had the first losing season in their history.

Graham turned down several coaching offers because he did not want the pressure or the lack of security. But he missed football, and in 1959 he became coach for the Coast Guard Academy in New London, Connecticut. For eight years, prior to the start of the regular season, he coached the College All-Stars in Chicago for their annual game with the NFL champions. In 1966, he signed a three-year contract as head coach of the Washington Redskins. When his contract expired, it was not renewed. Finally, he returned to the Coast Guard Academy to serve as athletic director.

In 1965, Otto Graham was elected to the Pro Football Hall of Fame, a fitting honor for a great quarterback.

Graham, coach of the 1958 College All-Star team, is carried off the field after the All-Stars defeated the Detroit Lions, 35-19.

⊕ Grange, Red (Harold) (1903-   ),

football player, was born in Forksville, Pennsylvania, and moved with his family to Wheaton, Illinois. An excellent athlete at Wheaton High School, Grange was a standout in basketball, track, and football. He was a state sprint champion and he thought that track would be his specialty at the University of Illinois. As a sophomore halfback in 1923, Grange led the Illini to an unbeaten season. The next year he scored five long touchdowns and passed for another against powerful Michigan. He completed his college career with 31 touchdowns and a reputation as one of the most gifted runners in history. Three straight years, Grange was selected as an All-American. In 1969,

when football celebrated its 100th birthday, Grange was named to every "all-time team" that was selected by different groups of authorities. Immediately after his college career ended in 1925, "The Galloping Ghost" signed a professional contract to tour with the Chicago Bears. His popularity opened the doors of pro stadiums to new fans in many cities.

Harold "Red" Grange's football career at the University of Illinois very nearly lasted only one day. Almost 300 freshmen had turned out for first-day football drills in 1922, so it was easy for one shy newcomer to get lost in the crowd.

Despite a remarkable record at Wheaton High School—where he scored 75 touchdowns (TD) and 82 extra points—Red Grange believed he was too small for college football. He turned out only because his fraternity brothers at Zeta Psi had insisted he do so. When those same brothers heard he had quit the team

as quickly as he had joined it, they persuaded him—with paddles—that football would be easier on him. He returned to the practice field the next day and launched the most publicized career in college football.

On the freshman team that fall, Grange caught the keen eye of head coach Bob Zuppke. After watching Red's blazing speed, feints, cuts, and quick starts, Zuppke reshaped the Illini offense to fit his future star. "I dropped my T formation and used what I called the Grange formation," Zuppke

said. He explained that Red would get in the set position about 5½ yards behind the line. It was a bit farther than usual, but necessary so that the blockers could get off their marks before the speedy halfback would run past them.

As a sophomore, Grange galloped into the national spotlight by leading the Illini to an undefeated season in 1923. In eight games he rushed for 723 yards (a 5.6-yard average), passed for 36 more yards, caught passes for 178 yards, returned interceptions for 140 yards, and carried back punts for 212

Grange, Red

yards. Against Illinois' easier opponents, Red played only partial games—once as little as 19 minutes. This fact makes these statistics all the more remarkable. At the end of the season, Grange was chosen All-American.

Despite the string of Illinois victories in 1923, a nagging group of critics belittled Grange and the Illinois team because they had not yet met Michigan, the most powerful team in the Midwest. Michigan fans—and even the Wolverine coach, Fielding Yost—hinted that

Red still had to prove himself on the gridiron. Red's chance came in 1924 when Illinois and Michigan met before a crowd of 67,000, the largest in the Midwest until that time.

Yost was smart enough to prepare for Grange, whom he had once tried to recruit. But he fueled the fire of the heated game by remarking, "Mr. Grange will be carefully watched every time he takes the ball. There will be about 11 clean, hard Michigan tacklers headed for him at the same time."

By carrying ice during the summer in Wheaton, Illinois, Red Grange earned the nickname of the "Wheaton Iceman."

Zuppke had been firing up his team for a whole year, sending his players letters all summer. By game time, they were ready to tear the Wolverines apart. But the clever Zuppke was not about to depend on spirit alone. He expected Michigan to try to cut off the speedy Grange on his long dashes straight down the sideline. Therefore, Zuppke ordered Red to cut back

toward the middle of the field the first time he got the ball.

On the opening kickoff, Red raced 95 yards to score. "It was the first time I cut back in my life," he recalled later.

He did more cutting that day. In the opening 12 minutes, he also made an end run of 56 yards, another of 67 yards, and still another of 44 yards—all for touchdowns. He had covered 303 yards in the short time span.

Red sat on the bench for the second quarter, but came back in to score another quick TD of 15 yards early in the second half. He also threw a TD pass. By the game's end, he had piled up 402 yards in the 21 times he carried the ball, and he had caught six passes for 64 more yards. The Illinois underdogs emerged the victors over mighty Michigan, 39-14.

After the account of this game appeared in the Sunday newspapers, Grange immediately became a new national hero. No one, before or since, ever put on such a dazzling performance in so brief a

Grange (second from right) signs a contract to play with the Chicago Bears in 1925. Owners Ed Sternaman (left) and George Halas (second from left) look on with C. C. Pyle, Grange's business manager.

space of time or in such an important contest. The Number 77 on his jersey became as famous as his name to fans throughout the country.

Grange was called on for more heroic feats two weeks later. His team was lagging behind a strong University of Chicago team, 21-0, when Red began to move. Soon

Grange, Red

A three-year All-America halfback at the University of Illinois, Grange later played professional football with the New York Yankees and the Chicago Bears.

The elusive open-field running of Red Grange, "The Galloping Ghost," haunted opposing teams and captivated football fans throughout the nation.

During a break in a Chicago Bears' practice session in New York City, Grange instructs a group of kids on how to carry the ball.

the score was 21-21 on three Grange TD's—the third one an 88-yarder around the end. The unstoppable halfback busted for another run of 50 yards, but it was called back. Illinois had to settle for a deadlock. In that Chicago game, he had passed for 177 yards in addition to the 300 he got running.

Grange ended his junior year as a unanimous All-America choice. In two years of college ball, he had scored 25 touchdowns and thrown for two more. He was probably the

greatest open-field runner in the history of football. Once he received the ball, he would dodge, weave, cut, and twist his way down the field, eluding the hands of tacklers like a phantom. This uncanny skill accounts for the nickname "The Galloping Ghost," bestowed on him early in his college career. The electric effect of his superb running lured thousands of fans to see him play at Illinois. The Illinois stadium came to be known as "The House that Grange Built."

Harold "Red" Grange was born in Forksville, Pennsylvania, on June 13, 1903. But he grew up in Wheaton, Illinois, where his father was the police chief. During Red's college years, he went back to Wheaton each summer to work on an ice truck to earn enough money to get him through another year at Illinois. Pictures of the "Wheaton Iceman" carrying huge chunks of ice through the streets made his new home town famous throughout the country.

The 1925 season was not as great as the others for Red. Many of his supporting cast of blockers from the 1923 and 1924 teams were gone, and Red himself had his share of injuries. Besides, the team needed him at quarterback. The Illini had lost games to Nebraska, Iowa, and Michigan when they went East for the first time in Red's career. "The Galloping Ghost" would have to prove himself to the Eastern sportswriters all over again —and he would have to do it against the East's best team, the University of Pennsylvania.

Franklin Field, home of the Quakers, was slippery that mid-fall day. But so was Red. He stunned the pride of the East with three touchdowns and 363 yards. The Illini smashed Penn, 24-2. Red had turned the Illini around in this game, and they finished the season without another loss.

But Red's 1925 season was far from over. A fast-talking promoter named C. C. Pyle had convinced Red to capitalize on his fame without delay. To do so, Red would have to turn pro as soon as his college season ended so that he could play in some more games during 1925.

Pyle did well by Red. He worked out a $100,000 deal with George Halas of the Chicago Bears for Red to go on tour with that team. They played several games,

"Number 77" leaves the field at Ohio State University after his last college game.

including eight within 11 days. In New York City, they drew 65,000 fans—the first major pro football crowd in that area. Pyle and Grange formed their own league in 1926, but it proved short-lived. They also went into other ventures —a movie and vaudeville. Later Red was successful in insurance, radio, and television. When his alliance with Pyle ended, it was estimated that Grange had earned nearly a million dollars.

Despite his great talent and fame, Red Grange was modest. Looking back over his career, he once said, "The guy who makes the touchdowns is very unimportant. It's a heck of a lot easier carrying that ball than blocking, believe me. . . . Nobody's great in football. You're only as great as the other ten guys make you."

When Red closed his active football career in 1935, someone totaled all his figures from high school, college, and the pros. It came to 4013 carries for 33,820 yards—more than 19 miles. He had averaged 8.4 yards each time he touched the ball and had scored 2366 points in 247 games.

But the figure that fans will remember most is "Number 77" from the jersey Red Grange wore. He wore it well.

♜ Graziano, Rocky

GRAH-ZEE-*AH*-NOH (1922-   ), boxer, was born Thomas Rocco Barbella in New York City. He was encouraged to box by relatives and learned many of his fighting tactics on the streets of the Lower East Side, the tough area where he grew up. Graziano spent eight of his first 21 years in reformatories and jails. In 1942, he won the 147-pound title in the Amateur Athletic Union (AAU) tournament. Later that year he began to fight professionally, but his personal troubles persisted. He had to spend 10 months in the Army stockade for being absent without leave (AWOL). He returned to the boxing circuit, scoring 25 knockouts in 46 bouts by the end of 1944. Graziano was knocked out by middleweight champion Tony Zale in 1946. The following year, he scored a six-round knockout over Zale

to win the middleweight crown. He lost his title to Zale in 1948. For the next few years, Graziano fought all the best middleweights in an effort to regain his title. His last try was against Sugar Ray Robinson. Rocky lost that one in 1952 and fought just once more. He retired with a record of 67 victories in 83 bouts, including 52 triumphs by knockouts.

Thomas Rocco Barbella was known to his buddies as Rocky when he was a boy on the streets of New York's East Side. He never dreamed he would someday be a champion boxer, rich and famous actor, entertainer, and TV personality. It seemed far more likely that he would end up like some of the kids around him. Several finally went to prison for life—four were sent to the electric chair.

Rocky Graziano (the name he later took) had more than his share of scrapes. He was a cocky juvenile delinquent, Army deserter, jailbird, and street fighter. But in the long run, his life straightened out. "Somebody up there must like me," he said many times during his ring days. The remark—slightly changed to "Somebody up there likes me"—became the title of his own book about his life. Later, a hit movie was based on the book.

Graziano's success story is unique. He was a fighter of limited talents—a good right hand was his main asset—but he rose to the middleweight championship of the world. He was a rough and uneducated man who mangled the English language, but he became a

A stinging right from Graziano jolts Charlie Fusari during their 10-round bout at the Polo Grounds in New York. The fight was stopped by the referee in the 10th round and Graziano was awarded a technical knockout (TKO).

Graziano, Rocky

popular TV personality when his fighting days were over.

His secret seemed to be his personal magnetism and natural charm. He had it as a fighter, and he kept it later when he got a chance to appear on TV. But in the beginning, all he attracted was trouble.

Thomas Rocco Barbella was born June 7, 1922, in New York City. Of the 10 children in the family, only five lived to see their teen years. Rocky himself was lucky to make it. Four times he was run over by cars. Once he fell down an elevator shaft. Another time he went through a plate-glass window, running from the police. He spent eight of his first 21 years in reformatories and jails.

Rocky's father and uncle had been boxers, and they encouraged him to spar with his brothers. A cousin, Lulu Costantino, was a pro and urged Rocky to try for a career in the ring. In 1942, Rocky entered an Amateur Athletic Union (AAU) tournament and won the 147-pound title. This drew the attention of several pro managers. But when they looked into Rocky's background, most of them were no longer interested.

But Irving Cohen, a mild-mannered little man from Brooklyn, thought Rocky had a chance. He tried to refine the kid's wild-swinging style. But before Cohen could sign him for a fight, Rocky was drafted into the Army and sent to Fort Dix, New Jersey, for training. In a short time, he was back at Stillman's Gym—where many fighters assembled—claiming he had been discharged. Actually, he had thrown a punch at his captain and walked out. To throw the military police off his track, he took the name and birth certificate of an old friend, Tommy Graziano, who was in prison.

In March 1942, he had his first pro fight, using his borrowed name of Graziano. He scored a second-round knockout. In the next two months, he fought eight times. Then the military police discovered that "Rocky Graziano" was really the Rocco Barbella they were hunting. Rocky was sent to the stockade at Fort Leavenworth, Kansas, for 10 months. "I guess I got some common sense there," he said much later. "I made myself a promise I'd never be locked up again." He never was.

In June 1943, he returned to New York and got busy boxing. Cohen booked 18 bouts in the next seven months. By the end of 1944, Graziano had scored 25 knockouts in 46 bouts, and he was the talk of the Brookyln boxing clubs. "Exciting but crude," the experts wrote.

The hottest middleweight at that time was Billy Arnold of Philadelphia. Graziano kept after Cohen

Graziano, Rocky

to get him a match with this "new Joe Louis." Against his better judgment, Cohen arranged the match in Madison Square Garden. Arnold had knocked out 26 of his 32 victims, and for two rounds it seemed that Rocky would also be one of Arnold's victims. But in the third round, Graziano nailed Arnold with a right to the chin, staggering him. Rocky followed up with three more knockdowns. "I told ya I'd beat the bum," Graziano crowed to Cohen and Whitey Bimstein, his trainer.

Rocky was on his way, running up a streak of eight wins with seven knockouts—including a second-round stop of welterweight champion Marty Servo in a non-title bout. When he went into the ring in Yankee Stadium on September 27, 1946, Rocky Graziano was a 3-1 favorite to dethrone middleweight champion Tony Zale.

Zale, 33, had finished four years in the Navy in January. But he was not as rusty as many had thought he would be. Zale floored Graziano in the first round. Then Rocky dropped him and Zale broke his thumb. The advantage see-sawed back and forth until the sixth round. Then Zale slammed a right to Rocky's heart and a left hook to the cheek. Rocky flopped onto the seat of his pants and stayed there for the 10-count.

The rematch went to Chicago because New York had banned

Lunging forward with a right to the stomach, Graziano went on to defeat Sonny Horne in a bout in 1946 at Madison Square Garden.

Rocky wipes his brow after testifying in a hearing before the New York State Athletic Commission in 1947. Having failed to report an offer of $100,000 to throw a fight, Graziano testified he considered the offer "a gag."

Graziano for failing to report a bribe offer for a fight that was never held. It was a record-breaking night in

Chicago—the temperature was 113 degrees at ringside, and there was a crowd of 18,547 paying $422,000. Zale, again the underdog, was in command for four rounds, flooring Graziano once and cutting him up. But in the sixth round, Rocky stormed out, shook up Tony Zale with a right, and pounded him on the ropes until the referee stopped the fight. Graziano had the title.

Briefly, the new champion's troubled past came back to haunt him. Details of his going AWOL (absent without leave) from the Army were brought out and the newspapers had a field day. But the public was behind Rocky. He was cheered by the crowd when he beat Sonny Horne in a tune-up bout. Graziano was favored to win over Zale for the third match of their series. The fight, held in Newark, New Jersey, on June 10, 1948, was completely in Zale's favor. A left hook sent Rocky crashing to the canvas, and one minute and eight seconds into the third round, Rocky had lost the title.

Not willing to retire, Graziano set out to reach the top again. In the next three and a half years, he fought the division's top men and ran up a long string of knockouts. On April 16, 1952, he got his chance to regain the title from Sugar Ray Robinson, the champion. Robinson knocked out Graziano in the third round. Graziano said once, "I'm one of the few guys who had Robinson on the floor—he tripped over my body.''

Graziano was ready to quit then, but Cohen suggested ''one more money shot.'' The opponent was Chuck Davey, a left-handed welterweight. Davey won on points in 10 rounds. ''I couldn't hit the guy at all, so I lost and I quit,'' said Rocky.

In 83 bouts Graziano knocked out 52 men, decisioned 14, won once on a foul, fought six draws, lost seven decisions, and was knocked out three times. He had become a rich man. ''My wife, Norma, made me stash it away,'' he said.

Then one day, TV writer Nat Hiken needed a former boxer to read a few lines in a show. Rocky Graziano's new career was launched. Now, his main interest is in the world of show business, advertising, and TV. ''I never had it so good,'' he admits. Graziano still, however, remains close to the boxing scene.

Writer W. C. Heinz described Graziano as: ''Exciting just walking down the street, and in the ring, the whole embodiment of what boxing is, which is fighting for the prize. Graziano's prize was the pass to get out of the East Side slum, the broken home, and the trouble with the law that were his heritage. For me, he put more meaning into a fight than anyone else I ever saw.''

⚾ Greenberg, Hank (1911-   ),

baseball player, was born in New York City. As a youngster, Greenberg had to overcome physical awkwardness and slowness before becoming an all-round athlete. Attending New York University for a year, Greenberg was more interested in sports. He eventually signed with the Detroit Tigers, who had pursued him since his high school days in the Bronx. Greenberg moved up to the Tigers in 1933 after three seasons in the minors. In about 10 years with the Tigers and one with the Pittsburgh Pirates, Greenberg became one of the outstanding right-handed power hitters in baseball history. He led the American League (AL) in home runs as well as runs batted in (RBI) four times. He became one of the first men to challenge Babe Ruth's season

record of 60 home runs when he smacked 58 in 1938. He almost matched Lou Gehrig's league runs-batted-in record of 184, but fell one short in 1937. During his career, Greenberg hit 331 home runs, had 1276 RBI's, and batted .313. In 1956, the former two-time American League Most Valuable Player (MVP) was elected to the Baseball Hall of Fame.

If ever there was a self-made ballplayer, it was Hank Greenberg. His youth had been spent in practice and more practice for the sports that he loved. It might be said that Greenberg's entire life has been built around the philosophy of hard work.

Although born to well-to-do parents, Greenberg never rested on that fact. He never took anything for granted, but instead worked hard to make himself the best at whatever he tried.

As a youngster, he was forced to overcome physical awkwardness to groom himself into a topnotch ballplayer. Later, when his athletic career was behind him, Hank Greenberg overcame a lack of education to become a success in the business world.

He is probably best remembered as the first man who gave Babe Ruth's single-season home-run record a merry chase when he belted 58 in 1938. But Greenberg was more than just a single-season wonder. He was one of the most feared right-handed hitters ever to play in the major leagues.

During his great playing career, from 1933 to 1947, Greenberg compiled a batting average of .313, belted 331 home runs, and drove in 1276 runs. These totals were gathered in a period of about 10 seasons, since Greenberg missed four and a half years while serving in the Army during World War II.

He gained repeated honors

Shown with some of his trophies, Greenberg holds the award he received as the Most Valuable Player in the Texas League in 1932.

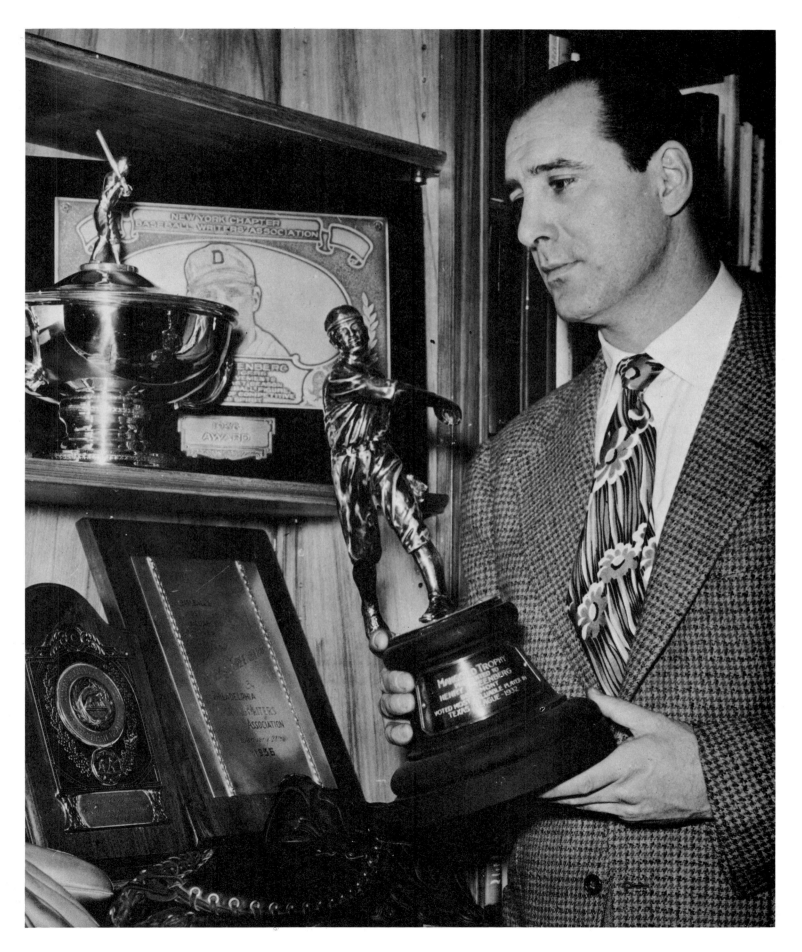

Greenberg, Hank

during his playing years. Greenberg tied the major and American League (AL) record for the most home runs in a season by a right-handed batsman. In 1937, he was second only to Lou Gehrig in runs batted in (RBI) for one season, 183. He set the major-league record for the most times two or more homers were hit per game in a season (11 in 1938). Greenberg, a member of the Hall of Fame, was also twice named the Most Valuable Player (MVP) in the American League.

Born on New Year's Day of 1911, Henry Benjamin Greenberg was the son of Rumanian-Jewish parents who had migrated to the United States from Bucharest. The family lived in New York's Greenwich Village until Hank was seven. Then they moved to Crotona Park, a wealthy section of the Bronx. Greenberg's father, David, was a hard-working man who had built a profitable cloth-shrinking business in Manhattan's textile district.

Greenberg attended public school No. 44 in the Bronx and played on his first baseball team there. Because he was big and slow and awkward, he was placed at first base. Hank was self-conscious of his size and gangly build, but he went at the game with tremendous drive and enthusiasm. Instead of retreating into a shell, he sought to improve his abilities. He wanted to be the best on the team and he worked hard toward that goal.

An excellent hitter during his career, here Greenberg awaits his turn at bat.

By the time he reached James Monroe High School, he had developed into a good all-round athlete. He starred for both the baseball and basketball teams and also played football and soccer.

While still in high school, he caught the attention of the pro scouts. He had reached 6 feet, 2 inches, and weighed 215 pounds. One of the scouts, Paul Krichell of the Yankees, told Greenberg that he had the potential to become a pro player. The quickly blossoming athlete wanted that more than anything, but his father planned for him to go to college first.

The Yankees offered Greenberg $7500 to sign with them, then Washington offered $12,000 and Detroit $9000. His father refused them all, insisting on college first. Detroit came back with another offer so that Hank could attend college first before signing with the Tigers. Finally, Greenberg's father

gave in.

In the fall of 1929, Greenberg enrolled at New York University on an athletic scholarship. By spring he realized he was not going to be able to finish school. Baseball meant too much to him, and he did not want to wait four years before he could play as a pro. His parents were disappointed but at last gave him their permission to report to Detroit.

In 1933, after spending three seasons in the minors, Greenberg reported to the Tigers' spring training camp. The manager of the Tigers, Bucky Harris, was not impressed by Greenberg's clumsy movements in the field. But as soon as the big man stepped into the batter's box, the frowns on Harris' face turned to smiles.

Realizing that the rookie's power could help the Tigers greatly, Harris placed him in the starting lineup. Greenberg responded by batting .301. By the next season, at 23 years of age, he had developed into a star.

Mickey Cochrane took over the Tigers as player-manager in 1934, and Greenberg enjoyed his first great year at the plate. Batting cleanup in a lineup that included Hall-of-Famers Charlie Gehringer, Cochrane, and Leon "Gocse" Goslin, Greenberg hit .339 with 26 homers and 139 RBI's. The Tigers won the AL pennant. In the World

Greenberg (right) presents President Harry Truman with an autographed baseball during a visit to the White House in 1946. Looking on at left is former Postmaster General Robert Hannegan.

49

Greenberg, Hank

Acknowledging cheers from the crowd, Greenberg takes the field for Detroit after hitting a three-run homer against the Cincinnati Redlegs in the fifth game of the 1940 World Series.

Series he continued to hit well, but the Tigers lost to the St. Louis Cardinals' famous "Gashouse Gang."

Detroit rebounded to win the 1935 world championship, and Greenberg was named the league's Most Valuable Player. He hit .328, with 36 homers, and drove in 170 runs during the regular season. He broke his wrist in the second game of the World Series and missed the final four games. But Detroit won despite Greenberg's absence, defeating the Chicago Cubs in six games.

The next year, Greenberg broke his wrist again in the 13th game of the campaign during a collision at first base. He missed practically the entire season. That winter, rumors began to circulate that he was through. The word was that his wrist was weakened for good and that his power was gone.

No rumor ever proved more unfounded. Greenberg came back in 1937 to drive in 183 runs. A year later, he made his spectacular try at Ruth's home-run record.

Actually, Greenberg had a great chance to break Ruth's record that year, but circumstances seemed against him. He had hit 58 homers in 149 games and still had five games left to hit three more home runs. Then, his luck turned. Batting against an erratic pitcher, a couple of wild ones, and—for the last double-header—dismal, darkening weather, Hank Greenberg missed his mark.

Greenberg had another big year in 1939. In 1940, he was suddenly shifted to the outfield to make room for Rudy York, a solid hitter who could not play any position but first.

After working hard to develop the skills needed as an outfielder, Greenberg was in left field on opening day. He finished the season with a lusty .340 average, 41 homers, and 150 RBI's to win his second MVP award. York's bat also contributed heavily, and the Tigers won the AL pennant again. But they were beaten by Cincinnati in a seven-game World Series.

Greenberg, by this time, was the highest-paid player in the majors. Then his career was dealt a blow in May 1941, when he was drafted into the Army. In December, though, he was given his release under a new government policy that permitted the discharging of men over 28. Greenberg was 30 at the time.

Then, two days after his discharge, the Japanese bombed Pearl Harbor. Greenberg re-enlisted as an officer candidate in the Army Air Corps. For the next four years, he served his country as a lieutenant and later as a captain.

Greenberg's first game after World War II was July 1, 1945, before a near-sellout crowd at Detroit's Briggs Stadium. The 34-year-old Greenberg was still in top physical form. But the fans wondered if he could still hit a baseball with the same power.

It did not take them long to find out. He homered during his first game back. In half a season, he batted .311, drove in 60 runs, and had 13 homers as the Tigers won the pennant. Greenberg followed that up by batting .304 with two homers and seven RBI's as the Tigers beat the Cubs in a seven-game World Series.

Greenberg's salary was raised to $75,000 for the 1946 season. When York was traded to Boston, Greenberg returned to first base. That year he led the league in homers (44) and RBI's (127), but it was his last at Detroit.

The Tigers shocked Greenberg and the entire baseball world the following year by waiving him, without notice, out of the American League to Pittsburgh. Although reluctant to play with the hapless Pirates at first, Greenberg agreed to go when they offered him $100,000—the first such sum in National League (NL) history. He was admittedly getting old and his feet were giving him trouble, but Greenberg helped the last-place Pirates at the gate that year. He hit 25 home runs and drove in 74 runs during 125 games.

Given his unconditional release in 1948, he then began working just as hard, with as much determination as a front-office executive. Later, Greenberg turned his talents to Wall Street. There, through shrewd investing, he became a millionaire.

Unlike many famous athletes, Hank Greenberg never suffered from want as a child. But he still worked with determination to become the best. And he proved that with hard work, the best can often be achieved.

⬤ Greene, Joe (1946-),

football player, was born in Temple, Texas. A standout at North Texas State University, Greene was a unanimous choice as the top defensive lineman in the nation in 1968. That year, he was a consensus All-American and the Missouri Valley Conference athlete of the year. In 1969, Greene was the number-one draft choice of the Pittsburgh Steelers, who were then in a rebuilding process. He soon became the finest defensive tackle in the National

Football League (NFL). He was selected the league's Defensive Player of the Year in 1972 and 1974. With "Mean Joe" anchoring the defense, the Steelers went all the way to win Super Bowls in 1974 and 1975. Combining speed, quickness, and strength, Joe Greene was an All-NFL choice every year from 1971 through 1976.

When Chuck Noll took over the head coaching job of the Pittsburgh Steelers in 1969, he wanted to rebuild the team, starting with the defense. So he chose a hulking tackle from North Texas State University in the first round of the National Football League (NFL) draft of college players. Noll passed over flashy running backs, quarterbacks, and receivers in favor of Joe Greene, who had torn apart college offenses in 1968.

While Noll's first Steeler team did not fare well—winning just one of 14 games—nobody criticized his top draft choice. In the coming years, it would prove to be one of the best picks in pro football history.

"Mean Joe" Greene, as he was nicknamed in college, became one of the greatest defensive tackles ever to play the game. And he anchored perhaps the greatest defensive front line ever, the "Steel Curtain."

While there was once a question of how good the Steelers would become when they gambled on Greene, there was little question of how good he would become. Joe was marked for greatness from the start.

Charles Edward Greene was born September 24, 1946, in Temple, Texas. The area was a hotbed of high school football, and Joe was one of the stars.

He attended North Texas State University in Denton, Texas. There, he was a member of a rugged defense nicknamed the "Mean Green" because of the team's green jerseys. Joe was the toughest member of that unit and he was tagged with the nickname "Mean Joe" Greene. It was something he later wished had never happened. He felt the nickname marked him as a dirty player.

At 6 feet, 4 inches, and 270 pounds, Greene was so strong and fast that he did not have to be dirty. He was so good that he was a three-time All-Missouri Valley

Surrounded by Cleveland players, Greene moves in for a solo tackle.

Greene, Joe

Conference tackle and an All-American in his senior year. He was also a unanimous choice as the best defensive lineman in the country and was chosen the outstanding lineman in the 1969 Senior Bowl.

The Pittsburgh Steeler scouts liked what they saw. Noll did not flinch when he made Joe his number-one pick to shore up the woeful Steeler defense. Some people questioned the choice, however. They wanted a flashy player, somebody who could make the game exciting.

The Steelers did not look good that first year. Even though Greene was all over the field, the defense gave up 404 points. But Joe got noticed. He was the Defensive Rookie of the Year.

In the years that followed, his nickname helped him become noticed by sportswriters and fans. And the fact that he got kicked out of a couple games for fighting helped make the nickname stick. Joe, however, tried to make people forget it.

"The Mean Joe Greene thing is not me and I really don't like it," he said. "When I first came up to the NFL, it was good publicity. But I've had a hangup about my size all my life. I don't want to be known as a bully.

"The nickname doesn't hurt me so much in the game as it does in my personal life. I like to think of myself as a nice person."

Once he joked that he was going to lose 20 pounds so people would call him "Lean Joe" Greene.

As his reputation grew, quarterbacks thought of Joe as being mean, but not dirty. He had become one of the best "sack" men in the game. In 1972, he tackled the quarterback 11 times behind the line of scrimmage. By that time he was an annual All-Pro choice. Greene was named the NFL's Most Valuable Defensive Player in 1972.

In the same year, the Steelers' defense held their opponents to 172 points. The club had become a playoff team, with an 11-3 record, and Joe Greene was the darling of Pittsburgh's fans.

Greene was so good that Noll allowed him to play wherever he wanted on defense in a game against the Houston Oilers late in the 1972 season. Joe roamed the field from sideline to sideline. He blocked a field-goal try, forced and recovered a fumble, sacked the quarterback five times, and made six tackles by himself.

Joe Greene (Number 75) congratulates linebacker Jack Ham (Number 59) on the sidelines. Once again, the awesome Pittsburgh Steeler defense has done the job.

Greene, Joe

"It was the best performance I have ever seen by a defensive tackle," said former Houston coach Lou Rymkus.

Greene was given the game ball by his teammates and later was named Defensive Player of the Week by the Associated Press. Houston scored only three points in that game.

"He is so outstanding that much of the time his play is taken for granted," said teammate Andy Russell, an All-Pro linebacker. Russell added that he could have played cornerback that day because Joe was making all the linebacker plays.

But Joe Greene was not satisfied with being a one-man show. He was quick to give credit to his teammates. It was Greene who once scolded fans for booing quarterback Terry Bradshaw when he was having a difficult time.

As Greene, Dwight White, Ernie Holmes, and L. C. Greenwood pulled the "Steel Curtain" down on opponents, Pittsburgh continued to win. The defense received much of the credit, and Joe earned all sorts of awards, including yearly All-NFL honors.

In 1974, Joe was superb. He was again the league's Most Valuable Defensive Player. He also led the Steelers to their first of two straight Super Bowl victories.

Prior to the 1975 Pro Bowl game, Greene relaxes on the sod in front of the other Steelers who made the AFC All-Star team. From left to right are Franco Harris, Andy Russell, L. C. Greenwood, Jack Ham, and Roy Gerela.

In the 1974 playoffs, the Steelers held the powerful Oakland Raiders to just 29 yards rushing. Oakland's running back Marv Hubbard said later, "Joe Greene comes off the line so fast that sometimes you don't even have time to close your eyes."

In the Super Bowl, Joe's pride was at stake because some people thought the Minnesota Vikings had a stronger defense. With the score 9-0 in favor of Pittsburgh, Joe intercepted a pass to stop a Viking drive. He later killed another drive on the Steelers' five-yard line when he pounced on a fumble. The Vikings gained only 17 yards in 20 carries that day, and Pittsburgh won the game, 16-6.

The 1975 season was more trying. Greene missed four games and parts of three others. But he still helped his team to a 21-17 Super Bowl triumph over the Dallas Cowboys.

In 1976, the Pittsburgh Steelers did not go all the way, but it was not because the defense slipped. The Steelers put together one of the greatest defensive seasons in football history. Many experts thought that 1976 was Greene's best year. The Steelers kept opponents away from the goal line in eight of their last nine games and recorded five shutouts to set NFL defensive marks.

Chuck Noll said it all when he remarked, "I've never seen a better defensive tackle, and he probably is the best defensive lineman I've ever seen. A fellow like Joe Greene doesn't run around blockers—he runs right through players."

Joe Greene (Number 75) has played in the annual Pro Bowl game several times. Here, he helps put a ferocious pass-rush on NFC quarterback Jim Hart.

The heart of Pittsburgh's "Steel Curtain," Joe Greene helped his team win two straight Super Bowl games.

Eyeball to eyeball with center Jim Otto of Oakland, Greene gets off the line as fast as anyone in football.

Greene breaks through the Oakland offensive line and sacks quarterback Ken Stabler.

⬤ Grier, Rosey

(Roosevelt) (1932-   ), football player, was born in Cuthbert, Georgia. His family moved to Roselle Park, New Jersey, where Grier became an all-round athlete at the local high school. He attended Penn State University, where he played football and put the shot on the track team. He was selected in the third round of the 1955 National Football League (NFL) draft by the New York Giants. In his second year (1956), Grier was selected for the All-Pro team as a defensive tackle after helping the Giants win the NFL championship. After spending 1957 in the Army, he returned to New York and stayed with the Giants for four Eastern Conference championships (1958, 1959, 1961, 1962). In 1963, the Giants traded him to the Los Angeles Rams. He continued

to be one of the biggest, strongest, and quickest tackles in the NFL. At Los Angeles he was a member of the "Fearsome Foursome," the defensive line that also included Merlin Olsen, "Deacon" Jones, and Lamar Lundy. Because of a ruptured Achilles tendon, Grier retired from football in 1967. Since then he has become a successful actor and singer.

At 6 feet, 5 inches and nearly 300 pounds, Roosevelt Grier was one of the biggest and strongest men in football. Grier was a first-rate tackle for the New York Giants in 1955 and 1956. After military service in 1957, he again starred with the Giants from 1958 through 1962. During his seven seasons in New York, he made the National Football League's (NFL) Eastern Division All-Star teams in 1956, 1958, 1960, and 1962. Grier also starred in the NFL championship games of 1956, 1958, 1959, 1961,

and 1962. In 1963, he was traded to the Los Angeles Rams. With them, he was almost an immovable blockade in the middle of the defensive line until he was seriously injured in 1967.

Not only did Grier help his mates with his play at defensive tackle, he also helped keep team spirit alive. He was carefree, the team humorist, and a man of warmth and feeling. He had the nicknames of "The Jolly Giant" and "Big Rosey."

Grier also proved he had other talents. As a guitarist and singer, he performed in Carnegie Hall and in nightclubs. After his football career ended, he became an entertainer and actor.

Roosevelt Grier was born July 14, 1932, in the village of Cuthbert, Georgia. Shortly after Roosevelt was born, the family of seven brothers and three sisters moved to Roselle Park, New Jersey. Young

Grier goes against two Detroit Lion linemen.

Grier, Rosey

With his eye on the ball-carrier, Grier doesn't seem fazed by this attempted block.

Roosevelt became an all-round athlete in high school.

When he was growing up, he was bashful and afraid to talk. But when he began singing, he lost his shyness.

Grier attended Penn State University, where he was almost as famous in track as a shot-putter as he was a football star. He heaved the iron shot-put some 58 feet and twice won the shot-put event in the Intercollegiate Association of Amateur Athletes of American (IC4A) meet.

Jack Lavelle, a New York Giant scout, and assistant coach Ed Kolman noted how Grier attacked opponents in football. They told the Giants they should make Grier an early-round draft choice. So, Roosevelt Grier was picked by the Giants on the third round of the 1955 draft.

Grier became one of the best defensive linemen in the league. He was large and strong and also had great speed. When he moved, there was a cat-like rhythm to his stride. His quickness and reaction enabled him to bring down smaller, faster men in the open field. "When Rosey's having a good day, there's not an offensive lineman who can handle him," said coach Allie Sherman.

In 1956, his second year, he helped power the Giants to the

Grier picks up speed in pursuit of a runner.

NFL title. His performance earned him All-Pro honors and a trip to the Pro Bowl.

Grier was drafted into the Army in 1957. Without Grier, the Giants' defense was weakened, and for one of the two times in seven years, New York did not win the Eastern championship.

But Grier was back with the Giants in 1958. New York again won the Eastern honors and repeated in 1959. They missed in 1960 but came back to win again in 1961 and 1962. In the 1962 NFL championship game, Grier overpowered Green Bay's offensive blockers and finally forced the Packers to direct their running plays at another part of the Giant defense. Even when the Packers put two men on Grier, they still could not stop his one-man attack.

Off the field, Grier was gentle in spite of his large size. Seldom was he seen without a smile. For relaxation, he did needlepoint with a master artist's touch. At training camp, Grier often woke the players at 6 A.M. with his voice practice. "I used them to try out new songs and arrangements," said Grier. "They didn't like it too much, but they figured they had to be out of the sack by seven, anyway. Finally, they told me I should get a job in a nightclub. So I did."

Grier began playing at a lounge not far from the camp, and

Grier, Rosey

While trying to block a Johnny Unitas pass, Grier meets All-Pro offensive tackle Jim Parker of the Baltimore Colts.

Jim Brown and Deacon Jones watch Rosey maul Cleveland Browns' quarterback Frank Ryan behind the goal line for a safety.

Grier puts on the "charge" against Philadelphia Eagles' quarterback Sonny Jurgensen.

Suddenly, and seemingly without reason, Grier was traded by the Giants to the Los Angeles Rams in 1963. The trade was for defensive tackle John Lovetere and a draft choice. Lovetere lasted only one year with the Giants, but Grier was oustanding with the Rams.

At the time of the trade, Grier was angry with the Giants' management. He was upset not only because it hurt his pride, but also he feared it would hurt his musical career. But he soon realized that there were even more nightclubs in Los Angeles than in New York.

In Los Angeles, Grier decided to lose some weight. He later recalled, "The first weight reduction method I tried was giving up water. I didn't touch a drop for 13 days. Next I tried starving myself. I ate nothing but peaches for six days. About that time a friend introduced me to Metrecal. It was a delightful little drink I had with each meal."

So then he went on his "teensy diet." "Before I invented it," said Grier, "I would try to lose weight by denying myself food until I thought I would go mad. Then I would cut loose and gobble up everything around.

"Well, by permitting myself 'teensies'—I mean tiny portions—I could satisfy my mind and not disturb my body. I used to eat a quart

his teammates liked to go out to hear him in the evenings. "I sang ballads and folk songs, like *John Henry and His Hammer.* I wrote many songs myself, such as *Let the Cool Winds Blow, The Mail Must Go Through,* and *Strutting and Twisting.*"

In the off-season, Grier played in nightclubs in the New York area. He had become a regular guest on TV shows.

A singer and musician, Grier performs at The Living Room, a nightclub in New York City, in 1963.

of ice cream covered with nuts. Now I have only one scoop with one nut on top.''

In September 1967, Grier was playing with the Rams against the Kansas City Chiefs. He dropped back to chase a Kansas City pass receiver. Suddenly, he felt pain in the back of his right leg, as if he had been clipped. He looked around, but no one was there. Then the 300-pound athlete went down in a heap.

The next morning, Grier was operated on for a torn Achilles ten-

don, a serious ankle injury. It was the end of his football career. But, the "Jolly Giant" was not overly sad about it because he could now spend all of his time on his career in movies and TV. Grier even regards his 1967 injury as a godsend.

He began to be known not only as a singer, but also as an actor. He played the role of sidekick to Daniel Boone with Fess Parker in the *Daniel Boone* series on TV, and appeared in movies as well.

But opposing players all agreed that Roosevelt Grier's impact on

the field was the thing for which he would best be remembered. "He'll never hurt you with a song," said Sonny Jurgensen, "but it's different when he belts you on the field."

Concerned with political and social issues, Rosey has long been involved in the battle for human rights. When Robert Kennedy was killed in Los Angeles, Grier was present as a member of his campaign. Later, he worked for Giant Step, an organization that helps the needy and underprivileged.

Griese, Bob

GREE-SEE (1945-),
football player, was born in Evansville, Indiana. He developed
his athletic talents at Rex Mundi High School in Evansville,
where he captained the baseball, basketball, and football teams.
Enrolling at Purdue University, Griese was selected as a football
All-American while only a junior. As a senior, he led Purdue to a
Rose Bowl victory over the University of Southern California.
The number-one draft choice of the Miami Dolphins in 1967,
Griese went on to set an American Football League (AFL)
record in his first year, completing 17 of 21 passes in one

game. After the 1971 season, *The
Sporting News* selected Griese as the
Player of the Year in the American
Football Conference (AFC). That year,
he guided the Dolphins to their first
Super Bowl. After recovering from an
injury in the 1972 season, Griese led
the Dolphins to a victory in Super Bowl
VII. The following year, Miami again
won the NFL title.

After an injury during the fifth game of the season, 1972 looked like it would be a disappointing year for quarterback Bob Griese. Although his team, the Miami Dolphins, was on its way to the first unbeaten, untied season in 30 years, he was not part of it. The young quarterback had to give way to veteran Earl Morrall. In Griese's absence, Morrall led the club to 11 straight regular-season victories and a playoff win over Cleveland.

But after Griese's long layoff, he came back strong in the second half of the American Football Conference (AFC) title game. He led Miami to a 21-17 victory over the Pittsburgh Steelers. Later, in the high point of his pro career, Griese led Miami to a 14-7 victory over the Washington Redskins in the Super Bowl.

In the title game against Washington, Griese regained his old form, out-thinking as well as out-playing his opponents.

From the Miami 32-yard line he noticed that the Redskin defense was overshifted. So he sent running back Larry Csonka up the middle for 13 yards. Washington compensated on the next play. Griese faked to Csonka up the middle and pitched out to running back Jim Kiick to the right. Because Kiick seldom ran pitchouts, Washington was caught off-guard and the play picked up eight yards. Aware of the single coverage on Paul Warfield on the third call, Griese faked to Csonka up the middle, faked a pitchout to Kiick, and then whirled and threw a 47-yard touchdown pass to receiver Paul Warfield. Although the play was nullified because Marlin Briscoe had moved before the snap of the ball, Griese continued to connect. Miami took a 14-0 lead when Griese fired a 28-

Leading the Dolphins to their second straight Super Bowl appearance following the 1972 season, Griese looks over the Washington Redskin defense while pacing Miami to a 14-7 win.

Griese, Bob

Bob Griese, then a star at Purdue University, passes under great pressure from Notre Dame defenders.

yard scoring pass to Howard Twilley in the first period. At the half, Griese had a six-for-six record in pass completions, gaining 75 yards. Keeping the lead in the last two periods, Griese finished the game with eight of 11 passes completed.

With the victory, Bob Griese had fulfilled all the expectations held for him when Miami picked him as their number-one draft choice out of Purdue in 1967. Even as a rookie, his worth was not doubted. He became a starter in the opening game of 1967 after regular quarterback John Stofa broke his leg. On October 29, 1967, he established an American Foo-ball League (AFL) record of passing efficiency in a game with 20 or more attempts. He completed 17 of 21 for a record of 81 per cent. In one stretch, he threw 122 passes without an interception.

By 1971, Griese had become the leading passer in the AFC. He threw 19 touchdown strikes and completed over 55 per cent of his attempts that year. *The Sporting News* named him the Player of the Year in the AFC.

After his superb performance in Miami's first Super Bowl win in 1973, Griese led the Dolphins to their second NFL title the following

Watching the action from the sidelines, Griese discusses strategy with Miami coach Don Shula (left) and reserve quarterback George Mira (center).

season. He took Miami to a 24-7 triumph over the Minnesota Vikings. In that game, he expertly mixed his few passes with a running attack.

"Passing is about 50 per cent of my game," said Griese. "I study as much on the running game as I do on the passing game. I talk to the offensive line coach as much as I do the receiver coach. A quarterback had better have an understanding of the passing game, but he also has to understand the running game. When to call the run is the thing."

Robert Allen Griese was born on February 3, 1945, in Evansville, Indiana. Young Bob was shaken severely in 1955 when his father, Henry, died. His mother sold her husband's plumbing business in Evansville and went to work as a secretary in order to hold her family together.

Grieved, Bob became somewhat of a loner. But he did find purpose and satisfaction in dedicating himself to becoming a successful quarterback. He was all-state his last two years in high school. More than 40 schools sought his services, but his choice—Notre Dame—

Griese rolls out to pass as Jim Kiick (Number 21) gets ready to provide some blocking.

Griese, Bob

Griese pitches out to one of his running backs

turned him down.

He then entered Purdue University and played both football and basketball. As a junior quarterback on the football squad, he was named All-American. That year, he completed 19 of 22 passes to upset the Fighting Irish of Notre Dame, 25-21. As a senior, Griese led the Purdue Boilermakers to their first appearance in the Rose Bowl, where they defeated Southern California, 14-13.

Since his entry into pro ball, Griese has played in four Pro Bowl games. Through 1976, he had tossed 139 career touchdown passes. He was one of the few NFL passers to complete 60 per cent of his throws in 1974 and 1975. But statistics mean very little in Bob Griese's case. He is a "thinking man's quarterback" who will get the job done in the most efficient way.

Bob Griese stays active away from the playing field. He is a frequent speaker and gives much of his time to charity. In the summer, he runs a boys' camp. He also plays golf, tennis, softball, and basketball—all to keep in shape for the football season.

Griese leaves the field on a stretcher after being injured in the first half of a 1972 game in San Diego. Dislocating his ankle and breaking a bone in his leg, Griese remained out of action until the playoffs.

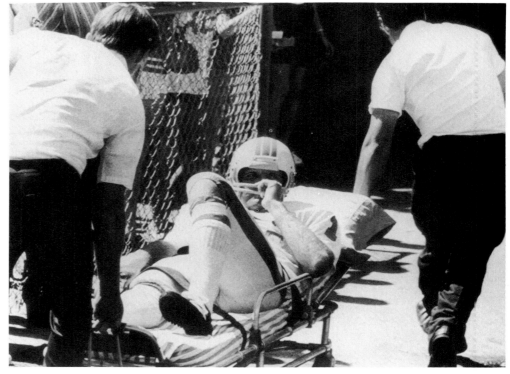

Resting briefly on the sidelines while the defense takes over, Griese and Paul Warfield discuss the Dolphins' passing attack.

Bob receives the snap from center.

Griese releases a pass despite being surrounded by Dallas defenders in the 1972 Super Bowl game.

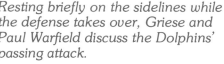

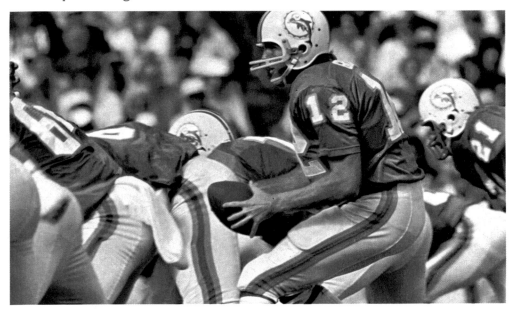

🏈 Griffin, Archie (1954-   ),

football player, was born in Columbus, Ohio. After starring in high school football, Griffin stayed in Columbus to attend Ohio State University (OSU). There, he became one of the greatest running backs in collegiate football history. In only his second game as a freshman, he set a school record by rushing for 239 yards. In the next three years, the 5-foot, 9-inch, 185-pound tailback gained well over 1000 yards rushing each season. For his play in 1974 and 1975, Griffin was awarded the Heisman Trophy as the outstanding player in college football. He became the first player in history to win the award twice. At OSU, Archie played in four Rose Bowl

games and set a National Collegiate Athletic Association (NCAA) record by rushing for at least 100 yards in 31 consecutive games. While some people thought he was too small to play pro football, the Cincinnati Bengals of the National Football League (NFL) drafted Griffin in 1976. He became a starter in his rookie year.

In the state of Ohio, where football legends are commonplace, Archie Griffin topped them all.

Born in Columbus, Ohio, on August 21, 1954, Archie Mason Griffin grew up in a football family. All seven boys played and loved the game.

As a boy, Archie would hitch-hike to Ohio stadium and try to get a free ticket to the Ohio State University (OSU) games. In Columbus, OSU football is so popular that tickets are hard to come by despite

the 86,000 available seats. The Buckeyes almost always have great teams to attract the many fans.

Ironically, a few years after he was asking for tickets, Archie Griffin was the star at Ohio State and made those tickets even harder to get.

Griffin starred at Eastmoor High School in Columbus, where he was named the best player in the state in 1971. After graduating, he chose to attend OSU even

though two older brothers played football elsewhere.

A new National Collegiate Athletic Association (NCAA) rule in 1972 made him eligible to play as a freshman. That ruling did not help Archie in his first game, or in the first six minutes of the Buckeyes' second game against the University of North Carolina. Head coach Woody Hayes was not going to play Archie. Then an assistant

Quick and elusive, Griffin picks up big yardage for Ohio State.

Griffin, Archie

In 1974, Archie Griffin received the Heisman Trophy as the outstanding college football player of the year. He was the first junior to win the award since 1963. He won the honor again in 1975, becoming the first player in history ever to win it twice.

coach convinced Hayes to play Griffin in that second game.

Griffin began running plays from the tailback position and began creating excitement for the Buckeyes. Before the day was over, he had rushed for 55 yards on one play, a touchdown on another, and 239 yards in all. That total was a school record. North Carolina coach Bill Dooley could not believe it. He had not even heard of Griffin.

In his first Big Ten game two weeks later, Griffin rushed for 192 yards against the University of Illinois. When the season was over, he had gained 867 yards. OSU fans looked forward to packing the stadium in 1973.

Coach Hayes fell in love with his new sensation. "Archie has great balance and unusual dedication and determination," he said. "He goes all out whether it is in practice or a game situation. We have never had a better football player nor have we had anyone as popular as Archie."

Those were big words for a 5-foot, 9-inch, 185-pound running back to live up to. But when Griffin rushed for 129 yards and brought two kickoffs back for 120 yards in his first game as a sophomore, there was little doubt left.

As the year progressed, Griffin gained over 100 yards each game. He got 246 against Iowa late in the season to break his own record. He gained 163 yards in the game against arch-rival University of Michigan and helped put Ohio State in the Rose Bowl. Archie picked up 149 more yards in the Rose Bowl to help the Buckeyes defeat the University of Southern California (USC), 42-21. Griffin gained 1577 yards in all as a sophomore. He was named the Most Valuable Player in the Big

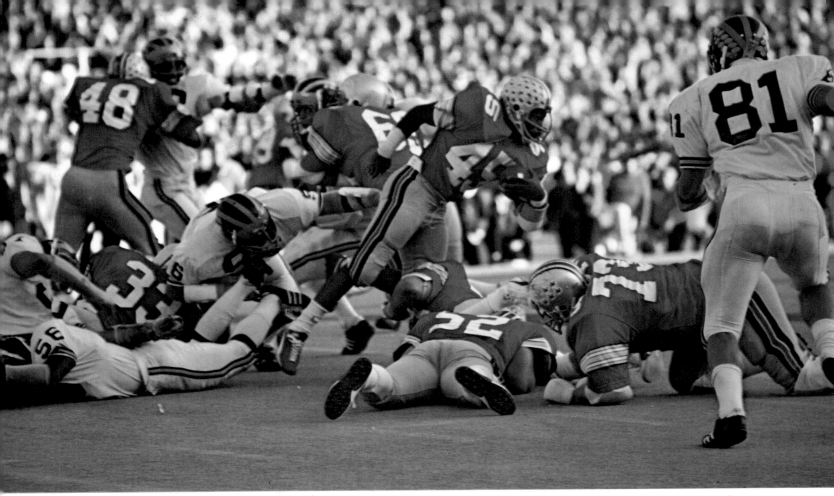

Griffin bursts through a gaping hole in the Michigan defensive line. The Buckeye offensive line helped Archie set collegiate rushing records at Ohio State.

Ten and an All-American.

As a junior, Griffin was never held below 111 yards in a regular-season game. He received the Heisman Trophy as the outstanding college player in 1975. He became only the sixth junior to win it in almost four decades. With 1620 yards rushing that season, Archie was quickly closing in on many NCAA records. In gaining over 100 yards for 22 straight season games, he had already set one record.

After he won the Heisman for the 1974 regular season, Griffin and the Buckeyes were stopped by USC in the Rose Bowl game, 18-17. The defeat gave Archie more incentive for his final season.

There was another incentive— no junior Heisman Trophy winner had ever repeated by capturing the award as a senior. In fact, no one in history had ever won the award twice.

But in 1975, Archie Griffin accomplished the feat. He ran his regular-season streak of 100-yard-plus games to 31 and totaled 1262 yards rushing for the year. He set NCAA career records with 5177 yards rushing and 6003 combined yards (rushing, receiving, and returning kicks).

Still, the pros were skeptical. Although Griffin had good balance, strength, and quickness, many thought he was too small to play in the National Football League (NFL). In the 1976 draft, 23 players were taken before the Cincinnati Bengals finally called out the name of Archie Griffin. The pressure mounted.

"I don't think anybody who won two Heisman Trophies could have come in and gotten accepted as well as Archie did," said All-Pro center and captain Bob Johnson of the Bengals. He added that Archie's attitude had helped.

Griffin started slowly with the Bengals and their pass-oriented offense. But in a mid-season game against the Kansas City Chiefs, Archie exploded. He churned for 139 yards on the ground, including a 77-yard touchdown run. It was the longest run from scrimmage in the American Football Conference all season. He finished the year with 625 yards rushing.

He had proved his critics wrong. He could play pro football and play it well. If his two Heisman Trophies were any indication, opposing NFL defenses would have their hands full when the ball was given to Archie Griffin.

⚾ Grove, Lefty (Robert) (1900-1975),

baseball player, was born in Lonaconing, Maryland. He played his first organized baseball game at 17 as a first baseman. Grove signed his first professional baseball contract with Martinsburg of the Blue Ridge League in 1920. Later that year, he joined the Baltimore Orioles of the International League. He led Baltimore to the Little World Series in his first year, and in the next five seasons compiled a 109-36 record with them. His first year with Connie Mack's Philadelphia Athletics was 1925. From 1927 to 1933, he won 172 games and lost only 53. In his greatest year (1931), Grove won 31, lost four, had an earned-run average (ERA) of 2.06, and tied an American League record with 16 consecutive victories. He was traded to the Boston Red Sox in 1934 when Philadelphia had financial difficulties. Grove finished his 17-year career with Boston in 1941. During his career he compiled 300 wins (20 or

more in eight seasons) against 140 losses. Grove also led the American League in strikeouts seven times and in ERA nine times. The man who led the Athletics to World Series victories in 1929 and 1930 was elected to the Hall of Fame in 1947, and was named the top left-hander of all time at the 1969 baseball centennial celebration.

Lefty Grove had an explosive temper and an explosive fast ball. Both have become legendary over the years, and both helped make Lefty Grove the best pitcher in the American League from 1926 to 1933.

Grove was a hot-tempered player who never knew how to lose graciously. But the fire within him helped make him the fierce competitor he was—though it did not help him build any lasting friendships with his teammates.

The fast ball was Grove's bread and butter. When he reared back and let loose, not even the great Babe Ruth could handle his whistling pitches.

For most of his career, Lefty Grove was lucky to have played on one of baseball's greatest teams, the Philadelphia Athletics of Connie Mack. That team was loaded with such Hall-of-Famers as Jimmie Foxx and Mickey Cochrane. Yet, Lefty Grove was such an overpowering pitcher that he probably could have been a big winner with any team.

During his 17-year big-league career, Grove had a record of 300 victories and only 140 defeats. In seven straight seasons, from 1927 to 1933, he won 20 or more games. Four times he had the American League's highest won-lost percentage, and nine times he led the league in earned-run average (ERA). His record is even more amazing considering that Grove never played an organized game of baseball until he was 17 and did not make the majors until he was 25.

Born on March 6, 1900, Robert Moses Grove was one of four sons of John Grove, a coal miner in Lonaconing, Maryland. While he was still very young, Grove went to work in the Georges Creek coal mines for 50 cents a day. Once, he said to his father, "Pop, I didn't put the coal in here and I don't see why I should have to dig it out." He saw no future in the work and left the mines before long.

With only an eighth-grade education, Grove took a job as a glass blower. After that, he worked for a time in the railroad shops in Cumberland, Maryland.

Grove played his first organized baseball game when he was 17 —as a first baseman for a team in Midland, Maryland. The coach soon noticed that Grove could throw harder than the pitcher, so Robert "Lefty" Grove became a pitcher.

In 1920, at the age of 20, Grove signed his first pro contract with Martinsburg of the old Blue Ridge League for $125 a month. Later that same year, the Baltimore Orioles, then a minor-league club, bought his contract for $2000.

Lefty Grove played 17 years with the Philadelphia Athletics and Boston Red Sox, winning 300 games.

Grove, Lefty

Grove led Baltimore to the Little World Series title that first year. Over the next five seasons, he compiled a 109-36 record. Several major-league clubs were interested in Grove during that time. But because Baltimore paid major-league salaries, Lefty was content to stay where he was. Besides, he still had not developed the control of his fast ball that later was to make him such a big winner in the majors.

In 1924, Connie Mack, owner and manager of the Philadelphia Athletics, decided it was time to take a chance on the hot-tempered left-hander with the blazing fast ball. So, he contacted his friend, Jack Dunn, owner of the Baltimore team. The two managers agreed on a price of $100,000 for Grove. Then Dunn had a thought. "Hey, Connie," he said, "let's make this a historic occasion. Add another $600. That will be more than the Yankees paid for Babe Ruth. It'll be baseball's biggest deal."

Grove's temper and his untamed fast ball got the best of him in his first year with the A's. He had the only losing season of his career. But Connie Mack was a kindly man who seldom raised his voice. He tried his best to settle young Lefty down. Mack was more successful at helping Lefty harness his control than he was at getting him to curb his temper.

Grove calmed down enough

Lefty poses with baseball's Most-Valuable-Player trophy, which he won in 1931. Grove won 31 games, lost four, and had an ERA of 2.06.

Baseball Hall-of-Famers Lefty Grove (left) and Bob Feller were picked as the greatest living left-hander and right-hander, respectively, by baseball writers and broadcasters in 1969.

to lead the American League in earned-run average in 1926. And in 1927, he won 20 games for the first time. From 1928 through 1933, Lefty was the leading pitcher in the league. He won 20 or more games in each of those seasons, while posting a combined record of 152 victories against only 41 losses.

In 1930 and 1931, Grove pitched the A's to two pennants in a row. His record for the two seasons was an incredible 59-9. In 1931, the A's pitcher probably enjoyed the greatest year of any major-league hurler. That season, he won 31 games and lost only four, while he racked up a league-leading ERA of 2.05. Three of his four losses that year were by one run, including a 1-0 defeat that snapped a 16-game winning streak. That was the game that brought on his most famous temper tantrum.

In that contest, the Athletics were playing the St. Louis Browns. Grove needed that 17th win to set an American League record for the most consecutive victories in a season. But he lost, 1-0, to a pitcher named Dick Coffman, who stopped the powerful A's on three hits.

Even worse was the way the Athletics lost the game. Al Simmons, the star left fielder, had asked Connie Mack for the day off because of an infected toe. Simmons' place in left field was taken by a rookie named Jimmy Moore. In the third inning, Fred Schulte singled for the Browns. Then Oscar Melillo hit a line drive to left field. Young Moore misjudged the ball and let it fall, giving Melillo a double. Schulte scored with the only run of the game.

After the game, Grove was

beside himself with anger. He tried to rip the clubhouse door off its hinges, he broke lockers, he threw his uniform on the floor and stomped on it. He swore at Simmons for taking the day off, and he swore at Connie Mack for letting him.

The Athletics lived with these angry outbursts for nine seasons. Even though Grove mellowed over the years, he never completely got rid of his hostility. Though he lost only 140 games in 17 big-league seasons, Lefty Grove thought of each one of them as if it were a terrible disaster. He constantly put down and badgered teammates for making errors. He would storm around the mound cursing whenever a batter was fortunate enough to get a hit off him. He would argue endlessly with Mack over the manager's decision in a close game. Whenever he lost a game, he would brood about it for days, refusing to talk to anyone. He was difficult with reporters, refusing to grant interviews with even the most famous sportswriters.

In 1934, Connie Mack had to break up the powerful Philadelphia team because of money problems. Grove was sold to the Boston Red Sox, where he pitched for another eight seasons. But he never reached the same greatness with the Red Sox as he had achieved with the A's.

The temperamental hurler be-

gan to have arm trouble, and he could no longer pitch his fast ball. But, he developed a fork ball and improved his curve. With these new pitches, he managed to win 20 games for the Red Sox in 1935. Years later, at the age of 39, he was still good enough to post a 15-4 record and a league-leading earned-run average of 2.54.

Lefty Grove continued to play major-league baseball until he was 41. He wanted to win the 300th game of his career. That came on July 25, 1941, when he beat the Cleveland Indians, 10-6.

One of the best batteries in baseball during the 1920's was Lefty Grove (left) and Mickey Cochrane of the Philadelphia Athletics.

Grove retired after the 1941 season, settled in Lonaconing, Maryland. There, he kept active in baseball through his work in the Little League program.

Elected to the Baseball Hall of Fame in 1947, he was named the top left-hander of all time at baseball's 100-year celebration in 1969. Lefty Grove died of a heart attack on May 23, 1975, in Norwalk, Ohio.

Groza, Lou (1924–),

football player, was born in Martins Ferry, Ohio. He began placekicking as a youth, booting the ball over telephone wires when he did not have access to goal posts. He captained the baseball, basketball, and football teams in high school, and he led the cagers to a state championship. Groza attended Ohio State University and played football there for a year before joining the Army during World War II. Then after the war, coach Paul Brown invited Groza to join his new pro football team, the

Cleveland Browns. Groza joined the team in 1946 and played with it until his retirement in 1967—except for one season that he sat out. Groza played a major role in the Browns' dynasty as both a kicker and offensive tackle. He established himself as the first of the famous pro placekickers. Lou "The Toe" Groza was inducted into the Pro Football Hall of Fame in 1974.

Long passes and running plays have made pro football America's most popular sport. But less dramatic place-kicks win games and championships. Lou Groza and his kicking skill helped transform the game of pro football and also made the Cleveland Browns a major football power for the 20 years he was with the team.

Lou Groza, the Browns' kicking ace, retired after the 1967 season. He had scored a career total of 1608 points. Until that time, no other player in the history of the game had scored so many.

This record number was surpassed four years later by George Blanda of the Oakland Raiders. But Groza's educated toe had shown

the way to a new style of play. His ability as a kicker of field goals and extra points convinced players, coaches, and fans alike that kicking could pay off. As a reliable point-maker in game after game, Groza changed the strategic concept of pro football.

In his earliest years, Groza usually had been called in to kick from a spot between the opponents' 30- and 40-yard lines. One Sunday, shortly after the Browns had joined the National Football League (NFL), they were at midfield on the third down with nine yards to go. Coach Paul Brown noticed Groza warming up.

"You want to try this distance?" Brown asked.

"Why not?" responded Lou.

After the third-down play, Groza went in and kicked a 49-yard field goal.

From then on the Browns became a scoring threat from midfield. Giving up the ball by punting on the fourth down at midfield almost went out of style in pro football. Lou Groza's great kicking had changed the strategy of the game.

Nicknamed "The Toe," Groza was one of the original members of the Cleveland Browns when the team was formed to play in the old All-America Football Conference

One of the greatest kickers of all time, Groza lines up a field-goal attempt during a Browns' practice session.

Groza, Lou

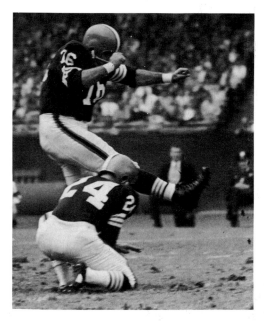

Groza's consistently great kicking earned him the nickname of "Lou the Toe." Here he is showing his excellent form.

New York Giant players put up their arms in a futile attempt to block a 39-yard field goal by Lou Groza of the Cleveland Browns.

in 1947. He spent 20 seasons as an active player. During that time, he chalked up a record of 810 extra points. He also held the record for the best percentage on field goals in one season—88.5 in 1953, when he hit 23 out of 26 attempts. The pre-World War II record for field goals by one team was 14 by the Giants in 1939.

"The Toe" helped the Browns win the NFL's Eastern championship in 1950 by booting two field goals in an 8-3 victory over New York. Then Groza's 16-yard field goal—with 20 seconds left in the game—won the NFL title for the Browns over the Rams, 30-28. After Cleveland's second touchdown that day, a low pass from center got away from Tommy James, who was holding the ball for Groza. With two minutes remaining, the Browns were trailing, 28-27. But Otto Graham rallied the team with short passes, bringing the ball nearer the goal line for Groza's winning kick.

The next year in the championship game, Groza booted a 52-yard field goal against the Rams. In spite of his effort, Los Angeles still managed to win, 24-17.

During one remarkable game against the Rams in 1952, Groza set a record by kicking on five plays in a row. In the final minutes of the first half, he hit a 49-yard field goal. Then he kicked off. The Rams fumbled the ball, and the Browns recovered. Groza kicked another field goal. He followed up with another kickoff on the final play of the half. Then he kicked off again to open the third period.

In 1954, Groza kicked three field goals in the title match at Detroit. The third, for 46 yards, put Cleveland ahead, 16-10. But late in the game, Bobby Layne completed a pass, making Detroit the winner.

Groza continued his outstanding kicks. During the 1957 season, he boomed five field goals of 50 yards or more in length.

Louis Ray Groza was born on January 25, 1924, in Martins Ferry, Ohio, a town of 12,000. Young men there either went to work in the coal mines or steel mills—or they played football.

Lou was the smallest of four sons, all of them active in many sports. Lou used to practice his placekicking over a telephone line at one end of a vacant field. Soon he was an expert kicker, weighing 210 pounds. Also a fine basketball player, Groza was a member of his high school's state championship team.

Groza attempts a field goal against the Baltimore Colts.

Many Midwest colleges wanted Lou to play for them. But he chose to attend Ohio State University, strong in both football and basketball. He played only three games for Ohio State's freshman team before going into the Army.

His tour of military duty took him to the Far East. During battle lulls, he still managed to kick a football in jungle clearings.

Coach Paul Brown at Ohio State kept in touch with Groza during these war years, writing to him and sending him football equipment. Brown wrote him about his plans for his Cleveland pro team. He pointed out that Groza could play pro football and in the off-season complete his college courses. Groza signed his contract with Brown while still on the battlefield.

Groza was mainly a kicker when he joined the new Brown team. But he also worked hard at offensive tackle and earned All-Pro honors at that position, too.

Groza sat out the 1960 season, then came back to play seven more years. He was 43 years old when he retired from football for good in 1967 after 20 seasons. No other player at that time had ever lasted so long in the rugged game. His ability to kick long and accurate field goals changed the whole style of play in pro football.

⊕Hagen, Walter (1892-1969),

golfer, was born in Rochester, New York. As a youth, Hagen participated in baseball as well as golf. He caddied at the Country Club of Rochester and later became assistant to the club pro. In 1913, Hagen tied for fourth place in his first tournament, the U.S. Open at Brookline, Massachusetts. He won the Open title the following year with a mark of 290 for four rounds. In the years to come, Hagen completely revolutionized golf with his showmanship, his colorful clothes, and his outrageous and carefree personal behavior. He was a golfer the general public could relate to. As a result, golf

became a national spectator sport and pastime. Hagen won the U.S. Open again in 1919; the PGA in 1921, 1924-1927; and the British Open in 1922, 1924, 1928, and 1929. In addition to these 11 major championships, Hagen won numerous other tournaments, including five Western Opens. He also played on seven Ryder Cup teams and was captain of the U.S. team in 1937.

Walter Hagen was one of golf's most famous names. He was also the most flamboyant pro ever to hit the tour. Sometimes he would report to the starting tee in a tuxedo. He often arrived in a limousine—drink in hand. Tournament golf was a lark to him. Hagen could never see why others choked up on the putting green. He did not even seem to care whether he won or lost—though he usually won. Walter Hagen advised other golfers, "Take it easy, relax, and laugh. As you travel down the road of life, you must smell the flowers . . ."

His casual manner toward the game did not hinder his power on the golf course. Hagen won the United States Open in 1914 and 1919; the Professional Golfers' Association (PGA) tournament in 1921, 1924, 1925, 1926, and 1927; and the British Open in 1922, 1924, 1928, and 1929—for a total of 11 major championships. He played on seven Ryder Cup teams and was captain of the United States team in 1937. He also won other tournaments, including five Western Opens. Only two golfers have since won more major titles—Bobby Jones and Jack Nicklaus.

In the 1920's, boxing had its Jack Dempsey, football its Red Grange, tennis its Bill Tilden, and baseball its Babe Ruth. But to the public mind, golfers were a stuffy lot. There was no popular hero. The sport needed someone different and attention-getting—yet someone who could win.

Golf found its man in Walter Hagen. He came to his early tournaments dressed in a coat the size of a pup tent, with his arm draped about a chorus girl and his free hand clutching a cocktail. As flashy as a neon sign, Hagen broke par and tradition with equal ease.

He was always charming, whether talking to British nobility or to the boys in the caddie shop. Nothing seemed to faze him. After winning the 1922 British Open (the first American to do so), Hagen, in a showy gesture, gave the first-place check to his caddie. Later, returning by ship to New York, he found he was broke. So, to tip his way off the boat and for cab fare to his hotel, he borrowed $25 from his teenage son. Hagen then rented an entire floor at the Delmonico Hotel to throw a big party for his friends. Luckily, one of them was rich enough to pick up the bills.

Hagen was one of the first men to use gamesmanship, although the term was not known in those days. He enjoyed "psyching out" his opponents and could handle them as well as he handled his clubs. One event showing his use of psychology came during the 1927 PGA at Cedar Crest Country Club, Dallas, Texas.

Hagen was defending champion. Though slightly off his game, he still managed to make it to the finals. Hagen's opponent in the finals was Joe Turnesa—who, at 26, was almost 10 years younger than Hagen.

The match was scheduled for 10 A.M., but Hagen did not arrive until 10:30. Turnesa began to tense up.

On the first hole, Turnesa's ball lay 10 feet from the cup. Hagen surprised the gallery, and especially Turnesa, by conceding the difficult putt. After 34 holes, Hagen was one down with only two more holes to play. On the 35th, Hagen's and Turnesa's balls were each about two feet from the hole. "You want to concede me this one, Walter?"

Among the leaders at the 1934 Masters tournament, Hagen attempts to drop a short but tricky putt.

Hagen, Walter

Hagen drives from the eighth tee at the 1934 Masters golf tournament in Augusta, Georgia.

Turnesa asked. Stooping to check the terrain, Hagen replied, "No, Joe, this looks a little tough. You'd better play it." Thinking the shot must be harder than it seemed, Turnesa nervously studied the green, choked up, and missed the short putt.

"Too bad, young fellow," Hagen said as he coolly tapped his putt in. Turnesa was, by that time, so tense he bogied the final hole. Hagen parred it to keep the title.

Walter Hagen once explained his feelings about golf to Grantland Rice, the leading sportswriter of the era: "I expect to make at least seven mistakes each round. Therefore, when I make a bad shot, I don't worry about it. It's just one of the seven."

Walter Hagen was born December 21, 1892, in Rochester, New York. As a boy, he was interested in both baseball and golf—teaching himself golf while working as a caddie at the Rochester Country Club. Andy Christie, the club pro, liked the boy's eagerness and energy, and young Walter became Christie's assistant. His main job was repairing golf clubs, but he found time to study the game carefully—learning different ways to grip the clubs for different shots.

In 1912, Hagen asked for time off to enter the National Open in nearby Buffalo. Christie agreed to let him go to watch, but not to play.

Walter Hagen takes time out between Ryder Cup matches in 1933 to sign autographs.

Hagen, Christie said, was not yet ready.

A year later, at 20, Hagen walked into the Country Club at Brookline, Massachusetts, where the Open was then being held. Sighting Johnny McDermott, the defending champion, and Francis Ouimet, he said, "My name is Hagen. I've come down from Rochester to help you fellows stop [Harry] Vardon and [Edward] Ray."

But it was Ouimet who did the stopping. In the three-way playoff, he shot a 72 to Vardon's 77 and Ray's 78. The newcomer from Rochester surprised everyone, though, by tying McDermott for fourth place.

In 1914, Hagen, dressed in a brilliant outfit, beat Chick Evans by one stroke for the National Open title. His mark (290) equaled a record set five years earlier. Later, he completely revolutionized golf by his colorful outfits and showmanship.

Hagen's extreme confidence never left him. Once, he and Joe Kirkwood, the trick-shot artist, stopped in New Orleans to play two local pros. Hagen asked what the course record was. Told it was 69, he offered to bet a thousand dollars he could break it. The money was

Hagen follows the flight of his drive.

quickly raised to cover the wager. On the last hole, Hagen rolled his second shot to 12 feet from the pin. He had to make the 12-foot putt for a 68. "You won't ever catch Mr. Hagen missing a thousand-dollar putt," he said as he sank the shot.

Hagen almost single-handed changed the status of professional golf. He was the first pro golfer to win more than $1000 in a single tournament. That amount is small compared to today's purses, but in 1915 it was an achievement. In

those days tournament purses on the golf tour were usually $5000 or less. On October 5, 1969, Walter Hagen died of cancer while at his estate in Traverse City, Michigan. But he left behind a lasting mark on the game of golf. His colorful personality helped make golf a popular and respected sport. His talent on the course is still honored. Early in 1973, a poll of national golf writers listed Walter Hagen as one of the five best golfers of all time.

⬤ Halas, George (1895-   ),

football coach and executive, was born in Chicago, Illinois. At Crane Technical High School, he was too small for football but starred in baseball. However, he did excel on the gridiron at the University of Illinois. After two years of Navy duty in World War I, Halas joined the New York baseball Yankees but only lasted a year because of an injury. In 1920, he joined the A. E. Staley Manufacturing Company in Decatur, Illinois, as athletic director. There, he put together a pro football team. Halas moved the Staleys to Chicago after the company phased out its sports program. The Staleys, later the Bears, were members of the original National Football League (NFL). It was through the efforts of Halas that the NFL was held together

in the early years. Halas coached the Bears until 1968—except for a few years off at different periods of time. Altogether he coached for a period of 40 years, winning five NFL titles (as early as 1933 and as late as 1963). Halas posted an overall coaching record of 321-142-31. In 1963, he was named to the Pro Football Hall of Fame.

The life of George Halas is the story of a dedicated pioneer. Through determination and hard work, he created the National Football League (NFL) and kept it on its feet during its early years.

One September day in 1920, in a Canton, Ohio, garage, Halas and a group of businessmen started the American Professional Football Association, later known as the NFL. Little did they know that four decades later the sport of pro football would turn into one of the world's most exciting spectacles.

Jim Thorpe was the first president of the new league, but from the beginning George Halas was the backbone.

Halas held the league together in the tough early years when Pete Rozelle was still a boy. He also did more than anyone else to popularize the game. He introduced the use of the spread end, created the man-in-motion strategy, and revived the T formation. He was the first coach to use movies regularly for spotting mistakes and plotting strategy. In 40 years as coach of the Chicago

Bears, he posted a record of 321-142-31 (.685) and won 91 more games than any other coach in pro football.

The fearsome reputation of the Bears, as well as the revival of the T, came largely in one game. It was the 1940 league championship contest when the Bears crumbled Washington at Griffith Stadium, 73-0. On the first two plays of the game, Halas

As a player, coach, and owner, George Halas has been a major contributor to pro football since its beginning.

Halas, George

Relaxing off the football field, "Papa Bear" Halas poses with a few of his trophies and awards.

Halas was a member of the 1919 New York Yankees before starting his football career.

sent Ken Kavanaugh to the left and put Ray Nolting in motion to the right. Immediately the world learned how threatening the T formation could be.

Football buffs in every city in the league retain a lasting mind's-eye picture of Halas as coach. Jaw thrust forward, hands deep in overcoat pockets, he would follow the ball up and down the field, yelling at the players, badgering the officials, illegally coaching from the sidelines. Attempting once to lend body assistance to a Bear field-goal attempt, he booted a big lineman right off the bench. When no time-outs remained, he would order some lineman to "go out there and get hurt." In the early days, he always wrestled with the fans for the football after conversion attempts.

Off the field, Halas was a to-

tally different person—gentlemanly, considerate, soft-spoken, poised.

But he could, in longshore-man's language, tear the hide off a huge but loafing fullback. Then he would send his victim back into the game, filled with murderous determination to smear the opposing linemen.

Late in the 19th century, George Halas' parents, both natives of Bohemia, arrived in Chicago with the floodtide of immigrants—Italians, Poles, Germans, Irish, and Swedes. There, George was born on February 2, 1895.

Halas' father was a tailor by trade, and to add to the family income, George and his two brothers were expected to work in their spare time. Since food was important to all immigrants, Halas

soon gave up his tailoring business for a grocery store. When it prospered, he began buying neighborhood houses. Each son was assigned to look after a house and collect the rent.

During his high school years at Crane Tech, George was too light for football. So he concentrated on baseball until his senior year. After graduation, he picked the University of Illinois because it had no tuition fee. There, he played football three seasons as a 170-pound end and also took part in baseball and basketball.

Graduating in 1918 with a degree in engineering, Halas at once enlisted in the Navy. Assigned to the Great Lakes Naval Training Station, he quickly became a star on its football team.

But there was no football team to join when Halas left the Navy. So in 1919, as a skilled outfielder, he accepted an offer from the New York Yankees baseball team. Then an injury in a spring game ended Halas' baseball career. He found himself replaced by a former Boston pitcher named Babe Ruth.

Halas turned to football and was an end for 11 seasons. He played with the Hammond Pros (1919), the Chicago Staleys (1920-1921), and the Chicago Bears (1922-1929). In 1923, the Bears played Jim Thorpe's Oorang Indians. Thorpe fumbled on the

After a 73-0 romp over the Washington Redskins in the 1940 NFL title game, Halas and the Bears celebrate.

Halas, George

Halas discusses game strategy at the blackboard.

water-soaked field at the goal line. Halas picked up the ball and outran Thorpe to the end zone. This run put George in the record book as the holder of the longest (98 yards) touchdown run made after a fumble. His record was not broken until 1972, 49 years later.

In 1920, in Decatur, Illinois, the Staley Manufacturing Company had undertaken a broad athletic program. The company offered Halas the post of athletic director, his main duty being to build a football team. Thus was born the team that eventually came to be known as the Chicago Bears.

In his new post, Halas put together a group of players that met the toughest clubs in the nation in 1920 and 1921 and posted a record of 19-2-3. Halas began to realize and dream of the possibilities in professional football.

By the fall of 1921, a poor business season forced the Staley Company to cut back its ambitious athletic program. With the company's blessing, Halas moved the Staley team to Chicago. As operating capital, George accepted $5000 from Staley's president in return for using the Staley name for a year. He took one of his Decatur players, Dutch Sternaman, as a partner.

Once in Chicago, Halas hustled ticket sales, along with his many other duties. The Chicago

Halas gives his star halfback, Gale Sayers, a few instructions during a workout.

papers ignored the club. But Bill Veeck, Sr., general manager of the Chicago Cubs baseball team, gave Halas the use of Wrigley Field for only a handshake.

The Bears did not really "arrive" until late 1925, when they signed up Illinois' Red Grange, the most exciting running back of the time. Grange's first pro game, against the Chicago Cardinals, packed Wrigley Field. Shortly after, Grange and the Bears played eight games in 12 days. Their first game in New York at the Polo Grounds drew 65,000—the largest crowd ever to see a pro game up to that time. On a later tour, they attracted 70,000 fans to see them play in Los Angeles.

C. C. "Cash and Carry" Pyle, Grange's manager, demanded a one-third share of the Bears in 1926. Refused, he created a rival league, awarding himself a New York team. The loss of Red Grange was a blow to Halas. And when the Bears slumped, Halas stepped down as coach. He hired Ralph Jones, one of his mentors at Illinois, as his replacement in 1930.

Jones brought the Bears the championship in 1932, when he had such awesome giants as Bronko Nagurski and George Musso—who, with halfback George Corbett, came up from Millikin University in Decatur.

Despite his new stars and the

Halas enjoys his 77th birthday cake, which was presented to him by federal judge Abraham Lincoln Marovitz, a friend of Halas for over 50 years.

return of Red Grange after Pyle's league folded, the Depression was closing in on Halas. Even though the Bears won the title in 1932, Halas lost money. Yet he never lost confidence. With help from Jim McMillen, a Bear great, and Charley Bidwell, later owner of the Cardinals, Halas bought out Dutch Sternaman's interest in the team.

Halas brought the Bears back, but it was not easy. After Halas had raised enough money to save his club, coach Jones resigned. Swamped by applications, Halas decided to coach the team himself in 1933. He spent the next 10 years as coach of the Bears.

The Bears captured the NFL title in 1933 by defeating the New York Giants, 23-21. Red Grange made the game-saving tackle on the last play.

The 1934 Bears were the best team ever not to win the title. With Nagurski running interference for quarterback Beattie Feathers, they went through 13 games without a defeat. Feathers was hurt before the playoff. But it was the frozen field, more than Feathers' absence, that beat the Bears in the playoff with the Giants.

Halas' next championship did not come until 1940, when he created perhaps the strongest 11 of all time. Sid Luckman was the perfect quarterback, and he fed the ball to such runners as Bill Osmanski, George McAfee, and Joe Maniaci. This was the team that murdered Washington in the playoffs.

The Bears were just as tough in 1941, when they signed two Stanford heroes, Norm Standlee and Hugh Gallarneau. They repeated as champions in 1941.

In 1942, the Bears had another fine season. Then Halas served in the Navy during World War II. At war's end, he returned to coach the Bears (except for 1956-1957) until 1968, when he retired.

Halas' last big season was 1963. The Bears posted an 11-1-2 record and won the NFL title. They beat the Giants, 14-10, for the championship.

In 1963, Halas promoted his son, George, Jr., to the posts of president, general manager, and treasurer, while he himself remained the Bears' coach and owner.

In that same year, George Halas was inducted into the Professional Football Hall of Fame. The choice was most appropriate, for without him, there would have been no Hall of Fame.

●Hall, Glenn (1931-), hockey player,

was born in Humboldt, Saskatchewan, Canada. He learned to play hockey on local outdoor rinks and tended goal for the junior team in Humboldt. After signing as a goalie with the Detroit Red Wings of the National Hockey League (NHL) in 1949, Hall spent six years in the minor leagues. In his first full year with the Red Wings, Hall led the league with 12 shutouts, had a 2.11 goals-against average, and won the Calder Trophy as the NHL's top rookie. He joined the Chicago Black Hawks in 1957. In the next 10 years, he was named to the NHL All-Star first team five times and to the second team three times. For four straight seasons (1960-1963), Hall led the NHL in shutouts. He was selected by the St. Louis Blues in the expansion draft in 1967-1968, and he received the Conn Smythe Trophy as the

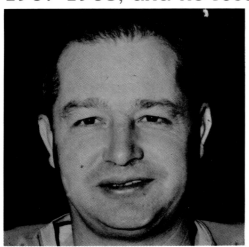

outstanding player in the Stanley Cup playoffs of that year. Hall played in an amazing 502 consecutive games from 1955-1962. Winning the Vezina Trophy as the goalie with the best goals-against average three times (1962-1963, 1966-1967, 1968-1969), he ranks second to Terry Sawchuk in all-time NHL games played (906) and shutouts (84) for goalies.

Glenn Hall described every game he played in the National Hockey League (NHL) as "60 minutes of hell." He ranked as one of the greatest goaltenders in the history of the game. But Hall played hockey as though in agony. At times, he was driven to such heights of anxiety that he vomited before games. Then, despite his upset stomach, he would go out and protect his cage like a man driven by frenzy.

"I'd sometimes ask myself," he recalls, "What the hell am I doing in hockey? But it was the only way I could support my family. If I could have supported my four kids some other way, you can bet I wouldn't ever have played goal."

For all his distaste, Glenn Hall played brilliantly for 16 seasons as a goaltender in the National Hockey League. He was the first goalie to reach the top salary level in hockey. In his final seasons with the St. Louis Blues, Hall reportedly received a salary of $47,500—the highest ever paid a goalie until that time.

Glenn Hall was well aware of the financial benefits in pro hockey. While he still was playing for the Chicago Black Hawks, he bought a farm 20 miles from Edmonton, Alberta. For several years, he and the Black Hawks' management had heated words over whether Hall would report for another season.

Glenn Hall gets ready in the St. Louis nets to hold off the Detroit Red Wings.

Hall, Glenn

Selected by the St. Louis Blues in the 1968 expansion draft, Hall went on to receive the Conn Smythe Trophy as the outstanding player in the Stanley Cup playoffs that year.

"I'm busy painting my barn," would be Glenn's reply late every summer when the Hawks would call to ask if he was planning to report. And each year—after he had played through his standoff—Glenn Hall would find the lure of the salary offered by general manager Tommy Ivan too much to resist. Then he would be back in the Chicago nets.

Hall suffered from a nervous stomach and general mental pain, two conditions that were not healthy for successful goaltending. But he managed to revolutionize the playing style for goalies—just as Bobby Hull's slap shot revolutionized offensive play in hockey. Before Hall, most goaltenders rarely left their feet to block shots. Bill Durnan of the Montreal Canadiens in the 1940's was the model of the stand-up goaltender, winning the Vezina Trophy six times using this style. Most young goalies attempted to copy Durnan's technique.

But Hall spent almost as much time on his knees as on his feet during his goaltending duties. When he went down to try to block a shot, his knees fanned out in a wide V formation and spread almost to the goal posts. In this position, his legs could protect against shots skimming along the ice. At the same time, his gloved left hand could catch rising shots and his stick hand could deflect them. This technique was particularly effective for Hall because he was so fast with his hands. Perhaps no other goalie ever was as adept at catching the puck as was Hall.

At the end of his career, Glenn Hall, who stood 5 feet, 11 inches tall and weighed 180 pounds, was turning gray at the temples. But he always wore a pleasant smile, setting off his deep-set brown eyes and unruly brown hair. His face, round and almost chubby in his youth, grew drawn and pale later in his goalkeeping years. His face also bore three prominent marks of the goalie's trade—an inch-long scar on the right cheek, another above the lip, and a third under the left nostril.

Glenn Hall established some incredible marks for tough and enduring goalkeeping. By his retirement after the 1970-1971 season, he had played in 906 NHL games, second on the all-time list to Terry Sawchuk. Hall's 84 shutouts also were second to Sawchuk's all-time 103.

In this sequence shot, Glenn Hall, as a member of the Chicago Black Hawks, shows his great goaltending ability. In the first picture he lunges for the puck. In the second and third shots he rolls over to make the grab. In the final photo he huddles around the puck to keep it from rolling into the net. The action occurred against Detroit in the 1961 Stanley Cup playoffs.

Oddly enough, Hall replaced Sawchuk as the regular goalie for the Detroit Red Wings in 1955-1956, following Sawchuk's trade to Boston. Many Detroit fans criticized the move. Sawchuk had just finished the 1954-1955 campaign, posting 12 shutouts and taking the Vezina Trophy. But the Red Wings, particularly general manager Jack Adams, were resolved to go with Hall.

Fred Pinkney was a scout for the Red Wings in Western Canada. He first spotted Glenn playing goal for the junior team in Humboldt, Saskatchewan—a railroad center in the heart of the province. There, Glenn Henry Hall was born on October 3, 1931.

Glenn first learned to play hockey on the outdoor rinks in his hometown of Humboldt, where the mercury often dropped to 40 degrees below zero. His father was an engineer on the Canadian National Railroad. And it is likely Glenn would have followed his father into railroading had he not chosen to be a hockey player.

After signing with Detroit, young Hall moved quickly through two years with the Windsor Spitfires in the Junior "A" Ontario Hockey Association. There, he was voted the Most Valuable Player in 1950-1951. Then he went up to the Indianapolis Caps in the American League in 1951-1952. Hall spent

most of the next three seasons with the Edmonton Flyers in the Western League.

During these years, Hall filled in for Sawchuk in the Detroit cage for eight games. He showed enough skill to justify, in the Red Wings' view, their trade of Sawchuk to the Bruins.

Hall fulfilled the trust placed in him. He posted a league-leading 12 shutouts and a standout 2.11 goals-against average in 1955-1956. He also won the Calder Trophy as the NHL's top rookie.

But Glenn fell out of favor with Adams the next year. After helping the Red Wings capture the 1956-1957 regular-season championship, Glenn and the rest of the club fell into a playoff slump. Detroit was knocked out by Boston in the first round. Before the next season, Terry Sawchuk was brought back from the Bruins to be the Red Wings' goalie again. Hall, despite being voted first-team NHL All-Star goaltender, was traded to the lowly Chicago Black Hawks.

With Chicago for 10 seasons, Hall became hockey's "Mr. Goalie." He was named to the All-Star first team of the NHL five times and to the second team three times. For four straight seasons (1960-1963), Hall led the NHL in shutouts. He also won the Vezina Trophy in 1963 with a 2.54 average in 66 appearances.

Hall, Glenn

Hall has to go high over the ice to deflect a Minnesota North Star shot on goal during the 1968 Stanley Cup playoffs.

Glenn Hall balked at signing with the first-year team, but the best salary offer of his career persuaded him to play. He was the main reason the St. Louis club reached the finals of the Stanley Cup playoffs against Montreal. Though the Canadiens swept the Blues in four games, each of the contests was decided by only one goal. Hall won the Conn Smythe Trophy as the outstanding player in the post-season competition.

The next season—when he was 37—Glenn teamed with 39-year-old Jacques Plante and again took the Blues to the Cup finals and captured the Vezina Trophy. Hall had also shared the 1967 Vezina in Chicago with Denis DeJordy. In that 1968-1969 campaign, Hall made the first NHL All-Star team for the seventh time on the strength of eight shutouts and a 2.17 goals-against mark in 41 outings.

Hall never lost his love for the western Canadian farmlands. Just before the 1972-1973 season, the Alberta Oilers of the World Hockey Association (WHA) lured him to join their organization, based in nearby Edmonton. But Hall remained only a few months before he told the Oilers he was going back to his farm—this time to stay.

In 1975, Glenn Hall was inducted into the Hockey Hall of Fame, located at the Canadian National Exhibition Park in Toronto.

That season of 1962-1963 also saw Hall sidelined for the first time in his NHL career. From the time he joined Detroit through the first 12 games of the 1962-1963 campaign with Chicago, Hall had played 502 games in a row. When the severe pressures of playing in the goal are considered, this 502-game streak is an almost unbelievable feat. What makes it incredible is that Hall played all three periods of every game—no backup goalie ever spelled him. In the game of November 7, 1962, at Chicago Sta-

dium (in what would have been his 503rd straight game), Hall started. But he had to be removed from the game against Boston because of a back injury in the first period.

Hall was brilliant in leading the Black Hawks to the 1960-1961 Stanley Cup title—their first in 23 years. But at the completion of a decade of service in Chicago, he was placed in the expansion draft pool when the NHL was enlarged to 12 teams in 1967-1968. Hall was selected by the St. Louis Blues.

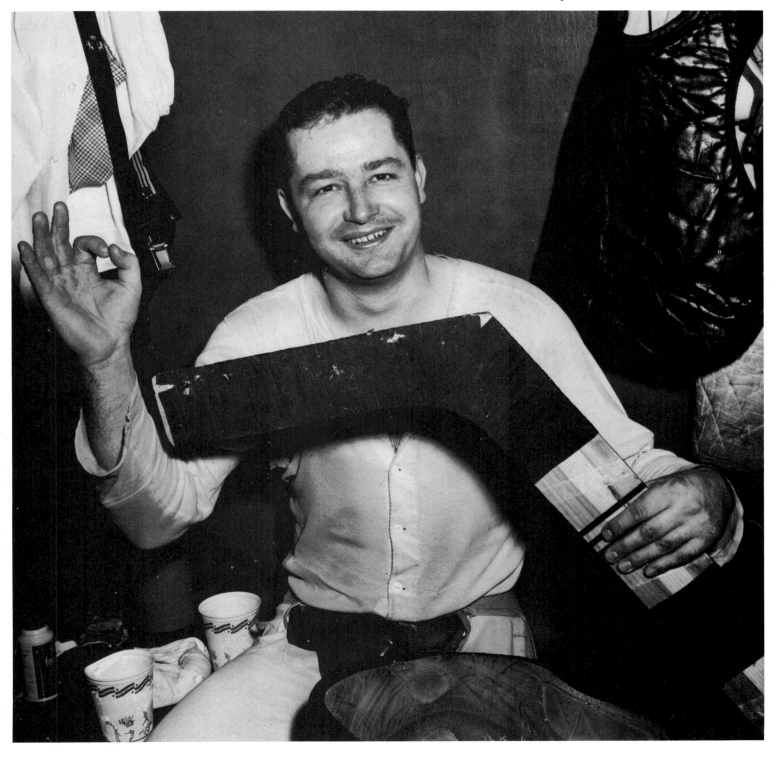

Glenn flashes a zero sign after he shut out the Montreal Canadiens in the 1962 Stanley Cup semifinals. Hall made 41 saves in the 2-0 Black Hawk victory.

⬤ Ham, Jack (1948-   ),

football player, was born in Johnstown, Pennsylvania. Though he played very little varsity football in high school, Jack later won All-America honors at Penn State University in 1970. He was the star of one of the best college defenses ever assembled. Partly because of his size, he was not drafted until the second round by the Pittsburgh Steelers of the National Football League (NFL). But he had no problem winning a starting job as a rookie and was named to the 1971 All-Rookie team as an outside linebacker. In 1972, Ham was an All-NFL

selection. That year, he had seven interceptions and four fumble recoveries. From 1974 through 1976, he was the only linebacker in the league to be selected to every All-NFL first team. Known for his quickness and agility, Jack Ham played a key part in Pittsburgh's Super Bowl victories following the 1974 and 1975 seasons.

One of Pennsylvania's greatest "natural resources" is its crop of talented young football players. Fortunately for the Pittsburgh Steelers, the state did not export Jack Ham. He has spent his entire career in his home state of Pennsylvania.

Ham is typical of the Pennsylvania-bred player—tough, determined, and dedicated. What he lacks in size, he makes up for in the way he plays the game.

Each time someone suggested he was too small, Jack Ham proved them wrong. In the end, his

mobility and intelligence helped him become the one of best outside linebackers in the game.

In the 1970's, zone defenses and lightning-quick defensive linemen prevented pro quarterbacks from throwing long passes as often as they had done before. More and more, quarterbacks were forced to throw to their running backs. Consequently, defenses needed fast and agile linebackers to stay with the running backs.

Jack Ham was one of those linebackers. His ability to anticipate

and come up with "the big play" helped Pittsburgh win two straight Super Bowls.

Born in Johnstown, Pennsylvania, on December 23, 1948, Jack Raphael Ham was just a fair football player in high school. It was not until his senior year at McCort High School that Ham got a chance to play—but it was halfway through the season. Though he was determined to be a college football player, no one was interested. Ham then decided to enroll at Penn State University. Meanwhile, his former high school team-

Dragging down a collegiate opponent, Jack Ham was an All-America selection while playing for Penn State University.

Ham, Jack

Ham makes a flying tackle on Cleveland's Leroy Kelly.

mate and budding Penn State star Steve Smear had talked to the Nittany Lions' coach, Joe Paterno. Steve told the coach about his friend Jack. Paterno had one scholarship left and he gave it to Ham.

Ham did not disappoint the coach. He lettered all three years as a linebacker and was an All-American selection as a senior. Jack was a star in the 1969 and 1970 Orange Bowls, and he played in two post-season all-star games.

At 220 pounds, Ham still did not have the size to impress the pros. When the 1971 National Football League (NFL) draft was held, Ham was not picked until the second round. He was taken by the Pittsburgh Steelers, who were then in the rebuilding process.

Jack was not sure of his future in the NFL. "I majored in business administration and I thought I'd just go out and look for a job like everybody else," he recalled. "I had it in my head that you had to be 6-foot-5 and 250 pounds for the NFL.

"I remember the first guy I met in training camp was Jon Kolb [262 pounds] and I shook hands with him and thought, 'What am I doing here?'"

In that 1971 rookie season, Jack proved what he was doing there. He earned a starting berth as an outside linebacker and also made the All-Rookie team picked by NFL sportswriters. With the game of pro football changing in favor of rangy outside linebackers, Ham found himself in a starring role.

"More than 50 per cent of the linebacker's responsibilities now are in pass coverage," he analyzed. "He [the linebacker] has to be fast and agile enough to cover the running backs coming out of the backfield."

That describes just what Jack did in his second season in the NFL. He intercepted seven passes to lead all linebackers in that category. He also pounced on four fumbles.

With his great mobility, Ham guards against the pass as well as any linebacker in football. Here, he stops Oakland wide receiver Mike Siani after a short gain.

Ham blitzes and sets his sights on quarterback Ken Anderson of the Cincinnati Bengals.

Ham moves in to lower the boom on a Philadelphia ball-carrier.

Playing for a team loaded with great defensive players, Ham began to shine as bright as any of them in 1974. On his side of the line, he had all-stars Joe Greene at tackle and L. C. Greenwood at defensive end. With Jack at the other linebacker spots were Andy Russell and Jack Lambert. The trio soon became one of the best sets of linebackers ever grouped on one team.

Jack was the quiet man on the team, but his actions spoke loudly. He intercepted five passes in the 1974 regular season and two more in the playoffs. He was an All-NFL pick for the third straight season.

And he was the only player at his position to be chosen on every 1974 All-NFL first team. More important, the Steelers won the Super Bowl, beating the Minnesota Vikings, 16-6.

Ham was a unanimous All-NFL choice again in 1975. In the playoffs, he made his biggest play of the year. Jack moved in on Baltimore quarterback Bert Jones and hit him so hard that he fumbled. Meanwhile, Andy Russell picked up the ball and ran it 93 yards for the crucial touchdown. From there, the Steelers went on to capture their second straight Super Bowl. When the season was over, Ham was chosen the NFL Defensive Player of the Year by *Pro Football Weekly*.

In 1976, the Steelers' defense was awesome. With five regular-season shutouts (an NFL record), Pittsburgh kept their opponents from scoring a touchdown in eight of their last nine games. That year, Ham brought his all-time Steeler interception record for linebackers to 19 in just six seasons.

"Even when Jack's on defense, he's on offense," said his coach, Chuck Noll.

While Ham did not talk much about himself, others did. "You don't get much of a chance to make interceptions playing outside linebacker," said Miami's Doug Swift, "unless your name is Jack Ham."

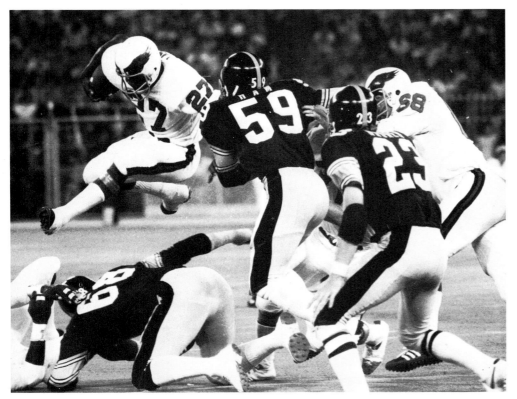

⛸ Hamill, Dorothy (1956-   ),

figure skater, was born in Chicago, Illinois. When she was about eight, Dorothy received a pair of skates for Christmas. She began skating on a frozen pond in her backyard in Riverside, Connecticut, where her family had moved. Inspired by the sight of more advanced skaters, she asked her mother to allow her to take lessons. Her obsession with skating was so great that she attended 5 A.M. training sessions at a rink. At 14, Dorothy dropped out of school and was privately tutored so that she could build her life around skating. In 1973, she was runner-up to Olympic star Janet Lynn in the

U.S. Figure Skating Championships. She won that title in 1974, 1975, and 1976. Dorothy Hamill won the biggest prize in figure skating in 1976—the Olympic gold medal. She captured the women's world figure-skating title shortly after the Winter Olympics. Dorothy then signed a $1-million contract to skate professionally for the Ice Capades.

It cost as much as $20,000 a year for Dorothy Hamill's family to develop her as an amateur figure skater. But young Dorothy showed her gratitude. At five o'clock every morning, she was on the ice, practicing the jumps, spins, and other maneuvers she had to master to become an Olympic champion.

Dorothy Hamill was born in Chicago, Illinois, on July 26, 1956. Later, her family moved to Riverside, Connecticut. When she was about eight, Dorothy was given a pair of skates for Christmas and tried them out on a frozen pond near her home.

Soon, she became envious of other skaters who could skate backward and perform other feats. She asked her mother if she could take lessons. Dorothy became one of the better figure skaters in her class. The pretty, brown-haired, blue-eyed girl was encouraged to concentrate on the sport.

That was fine with her. A few years later, Dorothy asked her school superintendent in Riverside to rearrange her class schedule. She wanted to devote as much of her time as possible to skating. For

each lesson, she had to be in a nearby town at five in the morning.

When she was 14, Dorothy dropped out of school to devote even more of her time to lessons, practice, and competition. Her parents provided her with private tutors so she could continue her education.

In 1973, Dorothy finished second to Janet Lynn in the U.S. Figure Skating Championships. Lynn had won the bronze medal

In 1976, Dorothy Hamill dominated women's figure skating.

Hamill, Dorothy

(third place) in the 1972 Olympics, and was about to turn professional. When Janet turned pro, American figure-skating officials looked to Dorothy to become the next champion.

Dorothy did not let them down. In 1974, she won the U.S. title at Providence, Rhode Island. By then, Dorothy had mastered the compulsory skating routines that are part of the scoring system. She still had trouble in the free-skating routines.

She won the U.S. Figure Skating Championships again in 1975 and 1976, and she was becoming a favorite of spectators and judges. Despite her free-skating flaws, she earned 5.8 and 5.9 scores out of a possible 6.0 in the January 1976 championships.

By then, Dorothy was a full-time skater. She had moved to Denver, Colorado, in order to be closer to rinks, competition, and a coach named Carlo Fassi. Fassi

For her artistic interpretation, Dorothy Hamill received a near-perfect score of 5.9 from each of the nine Olympic judges in free skating.

At the 1976 Winter Olympics in Innsbruck, Austria, Dorothy Hamill became a gold medal winner. She captivated the audience and judges with her beauty and style. After her final performance, which included the memorable "Hamill Camel," the crowd showered the ice with flowers.

A shy but happy Dorothy Hamill accepts her 1976 Olympic gold medal.

Clinching the 1976 Olympic gold medal, Dorothy performs her free-skating exercise.

During the Olympic award ceremonies for women's figure skating, Dorothy (center) waves to the cheering crowd with silver medalist Dianne de Leeuw of Holland (left) and bronze medalist Christine Errath of East Germany (right).

had also trained Peggy Fleming, the 1968 Olympic champion.

Under Fassi, Dorothy trained seven hours a day, six days a week. Dorothy was almost perfect in the compulsory events, where strict, rigid movements are necessary. For the free-exercise routines, she had become like a ballet dancer—able to suspend herself in the air as she twirled one and a half revolutions.

A judge at the 1976 U.S. championships said of her: "Dorothy skates with finesse. She performs a difficult program, works at high speed, plus she interprets the music with feeling. She is a beautiful skater."

Dorothy, in turn, said she was not always that way. "Before I got to Carlo [to train], I was tied up in a knot doing figures," she said. "I looked like a pretzel."

As good as she had become, however, the Olympic gold medal at the Winter Games in Innsbruck, Austria, was to be no easy task for Dorothy Hamill. For one thing, she had lost the world title in 1974 to Christine Errath of East Germany, and in 1975 to Dianne de Leeuw of the Netherlands.

Dianne de Leeuw actually lived in the U.S. but had citizenship in both countries. She decided to compete for her native Holland. She trained in the U.S. and flew off to Europe for the competition.

Hamill, Dorothy

Dorothy, realizing her own limitations, went to work the month before the Winter Olympics as she had never done before. "I worked the hardest I've ever worked this past month," she said. "My coach, Carlo Fassi, helped a great deal, and back on Long Island I was pushed very hard by my trainer, Peter Burrows, who really got me in shape."

When she took the ice at the Olympic arena in Innsbruck, she was ready. But Dorothy Hamill was not leaving anything to chance. Since it was Friday the 13th, she carefully pinned a gold four-leaf clover to the right shoulder of her outfit.

Until then, Dorothy had done very well—as expected. She had piled up the points in the compulsory figures earlier in the week. As she went into that Friday, February 13th, final event (the free-skating program), Dorothy was the 14th skater to take the ice. The other skaters would set the standards she would have to beat. Dianne de Leeuw would skate last.

Dorothy skated somewhat carefully to protect her lead. But she was graceful in her double jumps and spins. She was brilliant in a lay-back spin and in another looping movement that became known as the "Hamill Camel."

The crowd cheered loudly for her display of grace, beauty, and

After winning her third consecutive U.S. women's title in 1976, Dorothy gives coach Carlo Fassi a hug.

In 1976, Olympic champion Dorothy Hamill was honored by First Lady Betty Ford and the Women's National Republican Club in New York City.

talent. When she finished, the fans showered the ice with flowers. And the judges loved her, too. Each of them gave her a near-perfect mark

Before making her New York debut with the Ice Capades in January 1977, Dorothy checks out the hair style she helped popularize.

of 5.9 in artistic interpretation.

Dianne followed. Although she was unruffled by the cheers for Dorothy, Dianne could not match the performance. The final posted scores were 193.80 for Dorothy, 190.24 for Dianne. Dorothy Hamill became the fourth American to win the women's figure-skating competition at the Winter Olympics.

For Dorothy, who used to get up early to train, it was a night to rejoice. She wore the gold medal around her neck at dinner and stayed up until 5 A.M. When she went to bed, Dorothy put the medal under her pillow.

When the 12th Winter Olympic Games ended, Dorothy had another goal to shoot for—the world title, an event she had never won. She competed for the title in Göteborg, Sweden, a few weeks after the Winter Olympics. Dorothy won both the compulsory and free-skating programs. She became the first American to capture the women's world figure-skating title since Peggy Fleming in 1968.

In April 1976, Dorothy Hamill turned in her amateur status for a $1-million contract with the Ice Capades show. Performing all over the country, she became more admired all the time. Even her short hair style became fashionable. She appeared in her own television special early in 1977. Dorothy Hamill's hard work had certainly paid off.

⬤ Harmon, Tom (1919-   ),

football player, was born in Gary, Indiana. He attended Horace Mann High School, where he starred in basketball, baseball, track, and football. After receiving more than 50 college offers, Harmon chose the University of Michigan. From 1938-1940, he scored 33 touchdowns, 237 points, ran for 2110 yards (a 5.4 average), completed 100 passes for 1300 yards and 16 touchdowns, and also kicked extra points and field goals. He

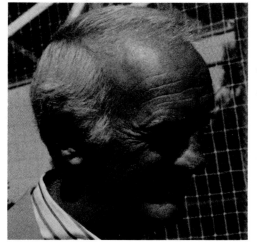

made everyone's All-America team in 1939 and 1940 and won the Heisman Trophy in 1940. Although he was hampered by leg injuries, Harmon played for the Los Angeles Rams of the National Football League (NFL) in 1946 and 1947. He accepted a job as sports director for a radio station in 1949 and has been in broadcasting ever since.

Harmon of Michigan—the name became as famous as Grange of Illinois. In scoring 237 points for Michigan between 1938 and 1940, Tom Harmon made 33 touchdowns, two more than Red Grange had tallied for the Illini team. In 1939 and 1940, young Tom Harmon was named to every All-America team in the U.S. He also won the Heisman and Maxwell awards for his skills as the best college player in America. For the record, Harmon ran for 2110 yards in 392 attempts, completed 100 passes for 1300 yards, kicked 33 points after touchdowns, made two field goals, and threw 16 scoring passes.

Paired with another freshman, Forest Evashevski, Tom began to make football history. With the huge Evashevski clearing the way, Harmon cut right through the Big Ten teams.

In the second game of the 1939 season, Michigan met Iowa, led by Nile Kinnick and his "Iron Men." That day Harmon scored all the points in Michigan's 27-7 victory.

On his 21st birthday, at the University of California in 1940, Harmon broke loose for four touchdowns, including runs of 94, 72, and 86 yards. He evaded every tackler, including an overeager fan who came plunging onto the field from the stands.

At the close of Harmon's last college season, offers poured in from all over the nation. George Halas had secured his draft rights for the Chicago Bears, and he told Harmon that he could write his own ticket. But Harmon turned down offers to play professional football in order to begin a career in radio. He had worked at radio stations while he was in school. And after graduating in 1941, he became sports director for radio station WJR in Detroit.

Tom Harmon played two football games in 1941—the East-West Shrine contest in San Francisco in January and the College All-Star Game in Chicago in August.

When he went to California for the Shrine classic, Harmon made a guest appearance on Bing Crosby's

In 1946, Harmon resumed his playing career with the Los Angeles Rams. This is his first professional game.

Harmon, Tom

Lieutenant Tom Harmon was one of the first P-38 fighter pilots in China during World War II. Reported missing on three occasions, the former University of Michigan star returned every time.

radio show in Hollywood. At Crosby's suggestion, Columbia Pictures made the movie *Harmon of Michigan*, with Tom Harmon playing himself. He made enough money from the picture to buy his parents a new home in Ann Arbor, Michigan.

During World War II, Harmon enlisted in the Army Air Force and became a twin-engine bomber pilot. Shortly after his parents had moved into their new home in April 1943, they received a telegram from the War Department that their son was missing over the South American jungle. A week later, Tom Harmon stumbled out of the jungle and into an Army camp. His plane had crashed, and Harmon was the only one of the five-man crew of his plane, "Old 93—Little Butch," to survive the ordeal of the steaming, snake-infested jungle. After recovering from his injuries, Harmon flew in North Africa. He then volunteered to join a group of fighter pilots being shipped to General Claire Chennault's "Flying Tiger" China command.

In November 1943, Tom Harmon was again reported missing in action. After 32 days, he was smuggled back to an American base by a band of friendly Chinese.

His plane had been shot down in an air fight with a pack of Japanese Zeros.

"I knew the Japanese used chutes for target practice," recalls Harmon, "so I tried to play dead. When I finally hit the ground, there were bullet holes in my parachute. The attack had been made well inside Japanese-held territory. I hid out for a while till my food gave out. Then I was picked up by a roving band who hid me and got me out intact."

On August 26, 1944, Tom Harmon married Elyse Knox, whom he had met in Hollywood. For her wedding, the bride wore a dress made of the parachute that had brought Harmon safely down from his burning plane over China.

Harmon was discharged in August 1945 with a Silver Star and a Purple Heart. When he received a $7000 tax bill from the Internal Revenue Service for earnings on his pre-war movie, Harmon began to play professional football. He accepted a $20,000-a-year offer from the Los Angeles Rams in 1946. The Rams had traded two players to the Bears, who held rights to Harmon. In two years with the Rams, Harmon was used on defense and offense. His nose was broken 13 times in 1947. In spite of his wartime leg injuries, Tom Harmon played well.

After the 1947 season,

After the final game of his college career in 1940, Harmon hangs up his famous Number 98 jersey. He had just scored three touchdowns in a smashing 40-0 Michigan victory over Ohio State.

Harmon became sports director for radio station KFI in Los Angeles. In 1949, he moved to the Columbia Pacific Radio Network as sports director. By 1962, he had joined the American Broadcasting Company (ABC) radio network, where he started a daily sports show. Tom Harmon and his crew cover many major sports events each year. He also handles national television assignments for the three major networks on a free-lance basis.

Tom Harmon rates as one of the coolest of sports broadcasters. Yet his voice throbbed with feeling as he described UCLA's early games of the 1972 season. During the opener, his emotions showed as he reported how his son, Mark Harmon, directed the Bruins to an upset victory over top-ranked Nebraska. He was also broadcasting the game against Michigan when Mark Harmon was injured.

Born September 28, 1919, in Gary, Indiana, Tom Harmon started competing in sports in grade school. At Horace Mann High School, he starred in football, basketball, baseball, and track. He pitched three no-hit games in a single season. He held the Indiana records for the preparatory school 100-yard dash and 200-yard low hurdles. In his high school senior year, Tom led the nation in scoring in football. Then from more than 50 college offers, Harmon chose Michigan and the legend began.

⬮ Harris, Franco (1950-),

football player, was born in Fort Dix, New Jersey. One of nine children, Franco was a high school football All-American. He attended Penn State University, where he rushed for 2002 yards and scored 24 touchdowns. Despite these impressive statistics, he was overshadowed by his teammate and fellow running back Lydell Mitchell. But the pros did not overlook the 230-pound Harris. The Pittsburgh Steelers made him their number-one draft choice in 1972. Harris rushed for 1055 yards in his rookie year—becoming only the fifth player ever to top the 1000-yard mark in his first season in the National Football League (NFL). He was named the American Football Conference (AFC) Rookie of the Year. As the Steelers became contenders, Harris

carried much of the team's offensive load. In Pittsburgh's first of two straight Super Bowl victories, Franco Harris rushed 34 times for 158 yards against the Minnesota Vikings in January 1975. He was chosen the game's Most Valuable Player. In four of his first five pro seasons, he gained over 1000 yards.

As Penn State University's fullback, Franco Harris was called on to block for Lydell Mitchell, the football team's game-breaking star. Franco was big then—6 feet, 2 inches, and 230 pounds—and a great blocker. Though he had his fair share of chances to carry the ball, it was Mitchell who received the acclaim. Franco gained 643, 675, and 684 yards as a three-year starter, but each season Mitchell gained more.

"I was used a whole lot for blocking," Harris admitted. "But I never resented it. Lydell deserved everything he got and more."

Penn State's offense was built around the running of such players as Mitchell and Harris. The big fullback was preparing himself for the pros anyway.

When the Pittsburgh Steelers of the National Football League (NFL) made Franco their number-

one draft choice in 1972, Harris began to see the light. "I matured mentally," he said. "I came to realize that natural ability is not enough. I found you have to have the frame of mind that you will do your best at all times."

There were many good backs available in that draft—including Mitchell, Robert Newhouse from the University of Houston, and Ed

Franco heads for the goal line.

112

Marinaro of Cornell. Chuck Noll, the Pittsburgh coach who was building a winner, wanted Newhouse, but owner Art Rooney could not help but be swayed by Harris' size.

"The big guys have longer and more consistent careers than the little guys," argued Rooney. The owner naturally won out. Franco Harris went on to change the history of the Pittsburgh Steelers.

Franco Harris was born on March 7, 1950, at Fort Dix, New Jersey, where his father, Cadillac Harris, was a mess-hall worker. Franco, the third of nine children, grew up with his large family in nearby Mount Holly, New Jersey.

Cad Harris, a black man, had met his Italian wife in Italy during World War II. Franco's mother, knowing little about football, did not want her son to play at first. His father did not know much about sports, so he did not push his son to play.

But Franco joined the junior high school team and later became a high school All-American back at Rancocas Valley Regional High in Mount Holly. He earned a scholarship to Penn State.

Harris gained a total of 2002 yards rushing and scored 24 touchdowns for the Nittany Lions while playing in the shadow of Mitchell and other Penn State All-Americans. He powered for two more touchdowns in the Senior Bowl All-Star game, impressing the scouts.

Franco was a little disappointed at being picked in the 1972 draft by Pittsburgh, because the team was not a winner. But once Chuck Noll began playing him regularly as a rookie, Harris changed his mind.

Harris started slowly, gaining just 28, 35, zero, and 16 yards in his first four games. Then he busted loose for 115 yards against the Houston Oilers, and everyone knew he was an NFL player.

He gained over 100 yards in seven games that year, including six in a row. He finished the season with 1055 yards rushing and a 5.6 average (tops in the league). Franco became only the fifth player to top 1000 yards in his rookie year. His six straight 100-yard games tied an NFL record set by the great Jimmy Brown, whose Number 32 Franco wore.

He was named the American Football Conference (AFC) Rookie

115

Harris, Franco

Harris weaves his way through the Minnesota Vikings' defense in Super Bowl IX. This run broke the Super Bowl rushing records for most carries and yards gained in one game. Pittsburgh won the contest, 16-6, and Franco was named the Most Valuable Player.

of the Year and also made the All-AFC team. He was the only rookie selected for the AFC team in the Pro Bowl game. More importantly, Franco Harris helped lead the Steelers to their first divisional title in the team's 40-year history.

In the playoffs, Harris shocked a national television audience when his team was trailing the powerful Oakland Raiders, 7-6, with just seconds to play. Quarterback Terry Bradshaw threw a desperation pass to Steeler running back John "Frenchy" Fuqua, but Jack Tatum of the Raiders deflected it. The Steelers' season seemed over. But Franco made a shoestring grab of the deflection and ran 42 yards for the winning touchdown. It was the first of many key games in which Harris came through gloriously.

Burly Franco Harris uses his great strength to shake a tackler.

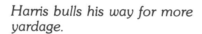

Harris bulls his way for more yardage.

The following season, 1973, he was slowed by a knee injury. He gained just 698 yards on the ground.

In 1974, Harris made a strong comeback despite a sprained ankle and bruised ribs. He rushed for 1006 yards and added another 200 yards on pass receptions. The Steelers made the playoffs again.

In 1976, Franco Harris became the Pittsburgh Steelers' all-time leading rusher.

High-stepping Franco Harris picks up 10 yards for Penn State University.

In the NFL championship game against the Minnesota Vikings, he set Super Bowl records by carrying the ball 34 times and rushing for 158 yards. He was easily the game's Most Valuable Player as Pittsburgh won, 16-6.

Harris' popularity grew in Pittsburgh, where championship football had eluded the city for so many years. Franco spoke to groups of city youngsters and helped out at local Boys' Clubs.

bus company even plastered its walls with the fact that Harris often used its transportation.

Franco loved the attention. "I think it's good because the people are enjoying it so," he said. "You have to evaluate it in the manner in which it's presented. Anyone can join and the people of this city can identify with this, Italian or not."

Blacks in Pittsburgh—also claiming the big fullback—formed "Franco's Black American Army" and had their fun, too.

In 1975, Harris gained 1246 yards—his best season yet. He also caught 28 passes and scored 11 touchdowns. He was an All-Pro selection again, and he helped lead the Steelers to the Super Bowl once more.

In Pittsburgh's 21-17 victory, he gained 82 yards. But it was his blocking and decoying that helped the Steelers beat the Dallas Cowboys for another Super Bowl title.

In 1976, the Steelers did not repeat their heroics—but Franco did. He gained 1128 yards and scored a career high of 14 touchdowns. He also set an NFL mark by carrying the ball a record 41 times in a crucial game against the Cincinnati Bengals.

Ironically, the old record of 40 was held by Lydell Mitchell of the Baltimore Colts—his former running mate at Penn State.

Meanwhile, Harris had become one of the city's biggest sports heroes. A large number of Pittsburgh fans were called "Franco's Italian Army" because of his heritage on his mother's side.

Harris earned his cheers in the 1974 playoffs. He scored three touchdowns in the first game against the Buffalo Bills. He then rushed for 111 yards in the AFC title game against Oakland.

Franco's Italian Army also began to grow. Fans began showing up for games in World War II helmets with the Italian colors (green, red, and white). The top fans were given military rankings, and even singer Frank Sinatra once joined the troops, much to everyone's surprise.

In downtown Pittsburgh, fans could buy a "Franco cocktail" and Franco Italian Army T-shirts. The

⌂ Hartack, Bill (1932-   ),

jockey, was born in Ebensburg, Pennsylvania. A year after graduating from high school in Pennsylvania, Bill began to work as a stablehand at Charles Town Race Track in West Virginia. Riding his first race for trainer Norman "Junie" Corbin, Hartack soon was winning races. In 1955, Hartack won his first national riding championship. He won the championship again in 1956, 1957, and 1960. Winning over 4200 races as a jockey,

Hartack rode to Kentucky Derby victories on *Iron Liege* in 1957, *Venetian Way* in 1960, *Decidedly* in 1962, *Northern Dancer* in 1964, and *Majestic Prince* in 1969. The second jockey to have won five Kentucky Derbies, Hartack also rode winners in the Preakness Stakes in 1956, 1964, and 1969, and in the Belmont Stakes in 1960.

Brash and testy Bill Hartack had little time to talk to reporters. He was too busy booting home winners from coast to coast, trying to prove that he was the best jockey in the world.

Hartack's intense desire to win has earned him a spot in thoroughbred racing history. Unluckily, he became a jockey about the same time another "great one" was breaking in—his name was Willie Shoemaker. Bill Hartack has had to live in the shadow of "The Shoe" for more than 25 years. But he is still out on the track whipping and driving his way to the winner's circle.

Hartack has won over 4200 races during his career. In his prime, he believed there was no better rider around. But he was not so much a boaster as a believer. His self-confidence enabled him to become one of the greatest jockeys in history.

He won national riding championships in 1955, 1956, 1957, and 1960, riding 417, 347, 341, and 307 winners in those years. After finishing second with *Fabius* in his first Kentucky Derby in 1956, Hartack came back the next year to win the "Run for the Roses" (Kentucky Derby) aboard *Iron Liege*. He beat Shoemaker and *Gallant Man* by a nose. But it was just the first of Hartack's Derby wins.

He won with *Venetian Way* in 1960, *Decidedly* in 1962, *Northern Dancer* in 1964, and *Majestic Prince* in 1969. Only Hartack and

the great Eddie Arcaro have won five Kentucky Derbies, the world's most famous horse race.

William John Hartack, Jr., was born on December 9, 1932, in Ebensburg, Pennsylvania. Bill's father worked as a coal miner. When Bill was eight, tragedy struck. His mother was killed on Christmas Day, 1940, in an automobile mishap. A year later the Hartack house burned down, and the family moved to a farm in Belsano, Pennsylvania. There young Bill attended Black Lick High School. He graduated at 17 in the top third of his class. Bill did chores around the farm as he

Hartack plants a kiss on Fabius, *after the two teamed for an upset victory over Kentucky Derby winner* Needles *in the 1956 Preakness Stakes.*

Hartack, Bill

Hartack weighs in at 114½ pounds before a big race.

waited for his 18th birthday so he could apply for a job at the Bethlehem Steel Company.

But one day Bill got a letter from one of his father's friends, asking him if he wanted to go to work at a race track. Bill decided to give it a try. He took a bus to West Virginia and the Charles Town Race Track.

Norman "Junie" Corbin hired Bill as a stablehand to muck out the stalls. Soon young Bill was helping to exercise horses in the mornings. Corbin could see that Hartack had a rare touch with a thoroughbred, and the trainer decided to put him up on one of his horses in a race.

"A week after he came I knew he had it," recalls Corbin. "I could tell from his nerves and those strong hands. Tell him something once and he'd learn it."

Hartack's first mount was *Hal's Pal,* and the young jockey was so nervous he forgot to put on his goggles. He finished last. Hartack was last again two days later on another horse, but Norman Corbin did not lose faith. Instinct told him to be patient with Hartack.

The next day Hartack rode *Nickleby,* a 9-1 shot, and won easily. Once young Hartack had won his first race, there was no stopping him. He won six more races in the next two weeks.

In 1953, Hartack started winning again. Before his 21st birthday, he had made enough money to buy his father a farm near Charles Town.

Owner Norman Corbin later sold Hartack's contract to Mrs. Ada L. Rice for $15,000. It was just the break Bill needed to make the big-time. Tommy Kelly trained the Rice horses, and one of them was *Pet Bully.* "*Pet Bully* was one of the key horses that I rode," said Hartack. "He got me into the stakes-rider class. I think I won about six stakes on him the first year."

Hartack's confidence was growing now. By 1955, he was the leading rider in the country. "I finally discovered that I knew what to do right," Hartack remembers. "I made all the right moves. I seldom made mistakes, and my reflexes have always worked to my benefit. Plenty of times you don't depend on what you think. Sometimes in a

Hartack and Majestic Prince drive across the finish line at the 1969 Preakness Stakes for another win.

Hartack, Bill

Hartack (center) rides Northern Dancer to victory in the 1964 Preakness Stakes. Northern Dancer, with Hartack up, also won the Kentucky Derby that year.

race you just don't have time to think. Then you depend solely on your reflexes. And I just happen to have good reflexes. You don't learn reflexes. You either have good reflexes or you don't."

Hartack was a picture of confidence in the saddle. But with reporters he was less sure of himself. With all his success the jockey got a lot of attention from newsmen. Questions seemed to upset the young athlete. Many times he did not answer them. Instead, he snapped back at the writers. Hartack was becoming his own worst enemy. His testy remarks only built up resentment on both sides. Hartack got mad and so did the people who had to put his name in the paper.

"My biggest problem isn't mounts, it's Bill's personality," said Chick Lang, who was Hartack's agent for several years. "I spend most of my time trailing around after him, apologizing to people he's insulted. He's particularly rude if he hasn't won."

"I'll tell you one thing," said Hartack, "if I was an owner or trainer, you know who I'd want riding my horses? Me. Because I want my jock, when he loses, to come back mad, just like me."

Hartack was not mad after the 1957 Kentucky Derby. That was the day he rode Iron Liege to victory after Shoemaker on Gallant Man misjudged the finish line and eased up. Hartack's face beamed with pride that day.

Hartack had won the Preakness Stakes the year before. He went on to win many big stakes after that, including the Preakness in 1964 on Northern Dancer and in 1969 on Majestic Prince. Bill Hartack's success made him rich. He bought a fine house in Hialeah, Florida, near the famous Hialeah race track.

He continues to ride at tracks all over the world. Perhaps fellow jockey Willie Shoemaker can best describe Hartack: "That boy has a lot of ability. A real good rider. He seems to have the knack of making just about every horse he rides give out with all the run that's in him—maybe it's a knack he was born with. Another thing, you've got to be impressed by the way he can keep a horse's mind on his work. He's a smart hand at keeping his mounts out of trouble, too, and at rating a horse—waiting for the right moment to start his move and saving something for the clutches, like they say in baseball.

"But maybe what would stand out most to many race-trackers about Hartack is his aggressiveness. He sure has the spirit for race riding, and I reckon it would be the same in any game he might take up. Aggressiveness and determination—and how he hates to lose! That hating to lose, I suppose, is as big a reason as any why he's one of the winningest jockeys that's come along in a long, long time."

Bill Hartack uses his hand to whip Majestic Prince (center) across the finish line to win the Kentucky Derby in 1969. Placing second was Arts and Letters (right).

●Harvey, Doug (1924-),

hockey player, was born in Montreal, Quebec, Canada. One of the few athletes to play in three professional sports, Harvey started his career by playing baseball. He later played minor-league football, but soon switched to hockey. His first professional hockey season was in 1947-1948, when he played in Quebec's senior league. After jumping back and forth between the minors and the parent Montreal Canadiens of the National Hockey League (NHL), Harvey got to stay up in the majors in 1948. He was always noted for his very casual style, but he often used it to lull opponents into losing the puck. Named to the NHL All-Star first team 10 times, he also won the James Norris Trophy as the best defenseman in the league seven times. Traded to the New York Rangers in 1961, Harvey played and coached. After spending a few years in the minor

leagues, he signed with the St. Louis Blues and led them to the Stanley Cup playoffs in 1969. Retiring at the end of that season, Doug Harvey had played in 1113 NHL games during his career. He returned to hockey as an assistant coach with the Houston Aeros of the World Hockey Association (WHA) in 1972. He remained with the club for three years.

Someone watching Doug Harvey play hockey for the first time might have concluded that he was a lazy player. In a sport where there is constant motion, Harvey's style was almost casual. He never appeared tense and he never appeared to be in a hurry. Often he purposely slowed down the game.

Harvey's style was so different, in fact, that he sometimes violated the rule of thumb that says you should never carry the puck close to your own goal—because an opponent might intercept and score a quick goal. Harvey would almost tease an opponent by dragging the puck in front of the goal. Then, when the opponent charged in to try to steal, Harvey would skate around him or pass off to a teammate.

For 19 years in National Hockey League (NHL) play, Har-vey was often the man who set the pace in a game. He was especially effective in the first 14 of those years, when he starred for the powerful Montreal Canadien teams. Though he may not have seemed to take the game seriously, he had a real love for hockey. He played minor-league hockey after his

Wearing the Montreal Canadiens' colors, Harvey (Number 2) steals the puck from two rushing Boston Bruins.

Harvey, Doug

major-league career seemed to be at an end, and he later made it back to the NHL after the league expanded.

Doug Harvey began playing hockey professionally in 1947 in the minors and closed out his career in 1969 with the St. Louis Blues, when he was 44.

Chasing the puck, Harvey (Number 2) hits the ice as a New York Ranger in 1963.

Douglas Norman Harvey was born in Montreal, Quebec, Canada, on December 19, 1924. As a youngster, he was an all-round athlete, starring in football, baseball, and hockey. Doug did not seriously consider hockey as a career then. He first thought about a future in pro football or pro baseball. He played minor-league football for a time with a team in

Montreal. But it was in baseball that he shined. He batted .342 in 1947 and .351 in 1948 for a minor-league team in Ottawa.

The old Boston Braves of the National League wanted to sign Harvey to a contract, but he balked at being sent to another minor-league club for further experience. Doug was already 24 years old, and he felt the time had come for him to get established in one sport. That was when he turned to hockey, a game he had been playing since he was 12.

By the time he was a teenager, he was spending much of his time at the game, playing for three teams in a single season.

Harvey started out as a center, but he soon learned that he could not skate fast enough to make it to the professional leagues at that position. So he switched to defense. The passing skills he learned as a young center, though, would help him throughout his career.

After playing for the Montreal Royals in Quebec's senior league, Harvey was promoted to the Canadiens for the 1947-1948 season. He failed to last in Montreal and was shipped out to the minors for more polishing. The next season, he went back to Montreal to begin a long stay in the majors.

At first, his teammates and members of other clubs were not

Harvey (behind the net) moves in to help his goalie Jacques Plante stop a scoring threat by Montreal's Jean Béliveau. Playing for the St. Louis Blues, both Harvey and Plante were former Canadiens.

quite certain what to make of the casual, self-styled player. Later, their respect for Harvey grew. As the 1940's came to a close, Doug was on his way to becoming one of the finest defensemen ever seen. At the end of the 1951-1952 season, he was voted to the All-NHL team, an honor he would receive nine more times—in 1953 through 1958 and 1960 through 1962. He was a second-team All-Star selection in 1959.

In addition, Harvey virtually had a lock on the James Norris Trophy, presented since 1954 to the man voted the best defenseman in the NHL. Harvey won it seven times in all.

Harvey earned the respect of his teammates for his unselfish play. He did not take many shots on goal. In fact, the most he ever scored in a single season was nine goals—in the 1957-1958 campaign. His coaches—first Dick Irvin, then Toe Blake—sometimes criticized him for his reluctance to shoot. But he maintained he would rather use finesse to work his way into shooting range and set up a goal for a teammate. "I didn't get a bonus for goals," he said one time, "so why not set up the guys who needed goals?"

Doug's style of play did not hold back the team. The Canadiens won five consecutive Stanley Cups from 1956 through 1960—an unparalleled achievement in major-league hockey. Harvey played for the free-wheeling teams that also featured high-scoring offensive stars such as Maurice Richard, Jean Béliveau, and "Boom Boom" Geoffrion.

Once the Canadiens were experiencing serious injuries to some of their star forwards. A Montreal sportswriter spoke to Lynn Patrick, a veteran hockey man, about the situation.

"Rocket Richard is hurt, Jean Béliveau is hurt," said the reporter. "Could anything hurt the Canadiens more than that?"

"Sure!" snapped Patrick. "Doug Harvey could be out of the lineup. Then the Canadiens would really be hurting."

Off the ice, Harvey was not always so popular. He did what he wanted to and sometimes that meant getting in trouble with the Canadiens' front office. He also disturbed the management by becoming involved in the organization of the first NHL Player's Association, a union, in 1961. In later years, his stubbornness may have been the reason that hockey officials were slow to consider him for the Hockey Hall of Fame. Later, the honor was bestowed upon him.

The Canadiens captured six Stanley Cup titles and were in the finals four other times during Harvey's years on the team. But that did not prevent the Canadiens from trading him to the New York Rangers before the start of the

In action in front of the New York goal, Doug Harvey (left) slaps at the puck to get it up-ice after the Red Wings had brought it near his goal.

1961-1962 season. Doug became player-coach of the New Yorkers, driving them to the playoffs for the first time in four years. He also won his seventh Norris Trophy for his defensive heroics.

But Harvey did not like the coaching half of his new job. He gave up the position after just one season. He continued to play for the Rangers, however, for two more seasons.

Then Doug drifted into the minor leagues. He played with five teams over the next few years. Then the Detroit Red Wings recalled him to the NHL for a couple of games of the 1966-1967 season. He took his minor-league role in stride after having spent so many years of stardom in the majors. "The money's not the best in the minors," he said. "But it's not the worst, either."

When the St. Louis Blues, an expansion team just one year old, signed Doug for the 1968-1969 season, they listed him as an assistant coach. The new team was not sure how much he could help them, considering his age and the fact that he showed only a shadow of his past ability. Much to the Blues' surprise, Harvey played 70 games. He gave the younger St. Louis defensemen valuable lessons. He also helped that team get to the Stanley Cup playoffs. Then he retired after the season, having played a total of 1113 NHL games. The unselfish Harvey had scored only 88 goals for all his 19 major-league seasons, but he had a sparkling total of 452 assists.

Doug stayed in the league as an assistant coach for a while, then spent a couple of years out of the sport. He returned to the game in 1972 as an assistant coach of the Houston Aeros in the World Hockey Association (WHA). He left the team in 1974 after the Aeros won their second straight league title.